FIRST
FUN
DICTIONARY

First published in 2001 by Miles Kelly Publishing Ltd
Bardfield Centre
Great Bardfield
Essex CM7 4SL

2 4 6 8 1 0 9 7 5 3 1

British Library Cataloguing-in-Publication Data
A catalogue record for this book is available from the British Library

ISBN 1-902947-82-7

Printed in Hong Kong

Author
Cindy Leaney

Editorial Director
Paula Borton

Project Management
Belinda Gallagher

Editorial Assistant
Mark Darling

Copy Editor
Margaret Berrill

Proofreader
Lynn Bresler

Art Director
Clare Sleven

Designer
Cathy May

www.mileskelly.net
info@mileskelly.net

FIRST FUN DICTIONARY

Cindy Leaney

Miles Kelly PUBLISHING

How to use your dictionary

Your dictionary is a book about words. It shows you how to spell words and explains what they mean. It also tells you how to use them. Many words will be familiar – the kind you use every day. Some will be new ones you are just beginning to learn. All are clearly explained. As you use your book you will find fun things to do and look at. Each letter of the alphabet has its own cartoon, and throughout the book there are puzzles, word games and fact panels.

Cartoons

When a new letter starts, look for the fun cartoons at the top of the page. These are brightly coloured scenes. See how many different things you can find starting with the same letter in each cartoon.

Did you know?

Look for the orange panels to find out interesting facts about the words in your book.

Alphabetical order

The words in this book are in alphabetical order. This means that all words beginning with A are grouped together, and so on. The coloured band along the bottom of every page will tell you which letter of the alphabet you are looking at.

Puzzle time

These are fun things to do and give you a chance to play with words. This helps you learn and remember them. All puzzle time activities are in green panels. These could be things like finding missing letters, word scrambles, matching pictures with words, or spot-the-difference games.

Entries

There are more than 1300 entries in your book. These are the words in **bold** type that you look up. For example, if you want to look up the word **plan**, go to the part of the book where the words begin with **p**. Look for the words that begin **pl**, until you find the word you want.

Definitions

Each entry is clearly explained, or defined.

place
where something is, the position, point or other location
There is a special place, deep in the forest.

plain
1 one colour, having no pattern or decoration
The curtains are plain green.
2 easy to understand
Can you tell me in plain English?
3 not fancy or complicated
It's a plain room, but very clean and neat.

plan
1 an idea about what will happen in the future
We have holiday plans.
2 a drawing of a room, building or other space
We drew a plan for our perfect playground.

plan (planning, planned)
to think about what you want to do and how to do it
We're planning a party.

plane
an aeroplane
The plane took off from the airport on time.

planet
one of the very large, round objects that moves around the Sun
There are nine planets in our Solar System.

Pluto

Neptune

Uranus

Saturn

Jupiter

Earth

Mars

Mercury

Venus

anets

plant
(planting, planted)
to put seeds or plants into the ground or containers so they will grow
Plant the seeds in early summer.

plant
a living thing that has roots, leaves and seeds and can make its own food
Water the plant every day.

plaster
1 a very thick paste which hardens when it dries
Plaster is used to cover walls inside buildings.
2 a thin piece of plastic or cloth that you put over a cut or sore
I have a plaster on my knee.

plastic
a light material that is made from chemicals
The bucket is made of plastic.

plate
a flat dish to eat food from
Take the plates into the kitchen.

plates

play
a story performed by actors in a theatre or on the radio
'The Tempest' is a play full of magical things.

play (playing, played)
to do things that you like such as games or sports
Let's play outdoors.

play

playground
a place for children to play
There are swings and a slide at the playground.

please
a word to use when you are asking for something politely
Please wait here.

plenty
enough or more than enough
Have one of my sandwiches, I have plenty.

plough
a piece of equipment that farmers use to turn the soil before they plant
Modern ploughs can cut through the earth very quickly.

plough

plug
1 a piece of plastic or rubber that stops water going out of a sink or bath
Put the plug in the bath, then turn on the water.
2 a piece of plastic connected to an electrical wire that you put into a wall
Which one is the plug for the computer?

plumber
a person whose job is to fix water taps and pipes
The plumber repaired the leak.

plus (pluses)
and, added to, the symbol +
Eleven plus six equals seventeen.
$11 + 6 = 17$
plus

pocket
a small, flat bag sewn into a piece of clothing or luggage
Put your key in your pocket.

poem
writing that uses words which sound good together. The words may rhyme
This poem is very funny.

Puzzle time

Here is a scrambled poem. Can you put each line in the correct order?
Hint — each line begins with a word that has a capital letter.

a. Roses red are
b. are blue Violets
c. sweet is Sugar
d. And are you so

answers
a. Roses are red
b. Violets are blue
c. Sugar is sweet
d. And so are you

a b c d e f g h i j k l m n o p q r s t u v w x y z 89

Illustrations and photographs

These also help you to understand the meaning of a word. Each illustration or photograph has its own label to tell you exactly what it is. Some of the illustrations are big and they may have several labels to tell you what different areas of the illustration are called.

Different forms of a word

Some of the entries are followed by the same word in a different form. The plural form is when there is more than one of something. Usually this just means adding an 's'. If a plural is more complicated than this, for example, the plural of 'knife' is 'knives', it is shown after the entry in smaller type within brackets.

If an entry is a verb (doing word) then other forms of the word will appear in the brackets. For example the verb **play** is followed by different endings, which appear in smaller type in brackets – **playing**, **played**. These show you when the action is happening or has happened.

Example sentences

These sentences follow the definition in *italic* type. They show you how you can use the word.

5

Aa

above
1 in a higher place
Annie lives in the flat above us.
2 more than
This ride is for children aged six and above.

accident
something that happens by chance
I dropped it by accident.

actor (actress, actresses)
a person who plays a part in a film or play
Charlie Chaplin was a famous actor.

▶ **actor**

add (adding, added)
1 to put something together with something else
Add the eggs, sugar and chocolate.
2 to put numbers together to find the total
Add six to four to make ten.

adult
a grown-up, not a child
Only adults are allowed in the pool after six p.m.

▲ **adult**

adventure
an exciting experience
Catching the plane by myself was a real adventure.

advertisement
words or pictures in a newspaper or magazine, or on television or radio, about things for sale
There is an address on the advertisement.

aerial
a piece of metal or wire for receiving or sending radio or television signals
There is an aerial on our roof.

aeroplane
a large machine, with wings and an engine, that flies
Sometimes aeroplanes fly over our house.
also look at aircraft

afraid
a feeling that something bad is going to happen
Are you afraid of snakes?

afternoon
the part of the day between midday and the evening
Let's go shopping this afternoon.

again
to do something once more
Can you say that again?

age
the number of years someone has lived.
At what age can I learn to drive a car?

aircraft
machines that fly
Helicopters, aeroplanes, microlights and gliders are kinds of aircraft.

airport
a place where aeroplanes land and take off from
The airport is very busy.

▼ **aeroplane**

alarm
a machine that flashes or makes a noise as a warning
The burglar alarm is flashing!

alien
something strange that comes from another planet
E.T. is a friendly alien.

▼ aliens

alligator
an animal with a long tail and big teeth that lives around rivers and lakes
Alligators lay eggs.

▲ alligators

alphabet
letters in a special order that forms a language
The English alphabet starts with A and ends with Z.

a b c d e f g h i
j k l m n o p q r
s t u v w x y z

ambulance
a vehicle for taking people who are ill or hurt to and from the hospital
Cars pull over to one side when an ambulance is coming.

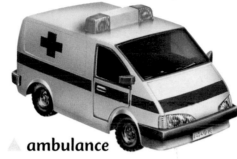
▲ ambulance

angry
a feeling that something is wrong or unfair
I am angry with you.

animal
a living thing that can move
Humans, fish, birds and snakes are all animals.

•Puzzle time•
Which of these animals is the odd one out?

a lion
b tiger
c snake
d cheetah

answer
c snake – it is a reptile

ankle
part of the body between the leg and the foot that bends
I have twisted my ankle.
also look at foot

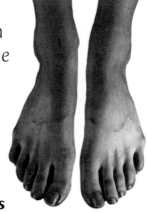
▶ ankles

answer
1 something you say or write after a question
My answer is no.
2 the correct reply to a question or correct result to a problem.
That's the right answer!

answer (answering, answered)
1 to say or write something when asked a question
You must answer the questions.
2 to pick up the telephone or go to the door
Answer the door!

ant
▼ ants
an insect that lives in groups
There is a line of ants marching into the sugar bowl!
also look at insect

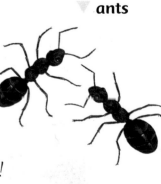

appear (appearing, appeared)

1 to look or to seem
She appears to be much better.
2 to come into sight
Our sister suddenly appeared.

apple

a fruit that grows
on trees
*Apples are red,
yellow or green.*
also look at fruit

◄ apple

apricot

a small, fuzzy yellow fruit
*I like dried apricots
on cereal.*

▲ apricots

apron

a piece of cloth that you put
on top of your clothes to keep
them clean.
*Put an apron on before you
open the paint.*

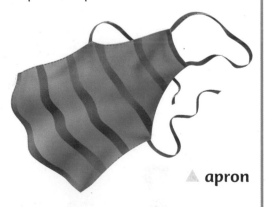
▲ apron

aquarium

a plastic or glass box filled
with water for keeping fish in
The fish swim in the aquarium.

·Puzzle time·

Can you untangle the lines to see
which fish has eaten the worm?

argue (arguing, argued)

to strongly disagree
Don't argue, it's not important.

arm

part of your body between
your shoulder and hand
*My right arm is stronger than
my left arm.*

armchair

a chair with places to rest
your arms
I like to read in an armchair.
also look at chair

army

the people that fight for a
country on land
*The Roman army was very
powerful.*

arrest (arresting, arrested)

to take someone away and
guard them
The police arrested two people.

art

the making of paintings,
drawings and sculpture
There is an art show at school.

artist

a person who makes art
Picasso is a famous artist.

▲ artist

ask (asking, asked)

to say to someone you want
them to tell you something,
or do something for you
You should ask for help.

asleep

sleeping
Shhh, she is fast asleep.

⬛ asleep

astronaut

a person who travels into space in a spacecraft
Astronauts sometimes spend months on a space station.

⬛ astronaut

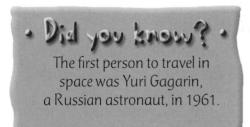

· Did you know? ·
The first person to travel in space was Yuri Gagarin, a Russian astronaut, in 1961.

athlete

a person who plays a sport.
Athletes train every day.
also look at sport

⬛ athlete

attack (attacking, attacked)

to be violent
Pirates attacked the ship.

aunt

the sister of your mother or father, the wife of your uncle
My aunt looks like my mother.
also look at family

autograph

the name of a famous person, written by them
Can I have your autograph?

automatic

a machine that works by itself
The washing machine is automatic.

autumn

the time of year between the summer and the winter
The leaves turn red in autumn.

⬛ autumn

awake

not sleeping, not asleep
I tried to stay awake all night.

awful

very bad
This medicine tastes awful.

axe

a tool with a handle and a sharp piece of metal at the end that is used for chopping wood and cutting down trees
Dad uses an axe to chop wood.

⬛ axe

Bb

baboon
a large monkey
Baboons are very noisy.

baby (babies)
a young child that has not yet learned to talk or walk
The baby's name is Alex.

▶ **baby**

back
1 part of your body behind you, between your shoulders and hips
I can swim on my back.
2 the part of something that is furthest from the front or from the way it is facing
The wires are at the back of the computer.

backwards
the direction opposite to the way something is facing
Take four steps backwards.

bacon
meat from a pig
We have bacon and eggs for breakfast.

bad (worse, worst)
not good or pleasant
The weather is very bad.

badge
a piece of paper, plastic, metal or cloth that you put on your clothes to say who you are or what you have done
I have four swimming badges.

badger
an animal with black and white fur that lives underground
There is a family of badgers living in the wood.

▽ **badger**

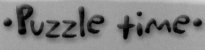

•Puzzle time•
These words are written backwards. Can you tell what they say?

tahw a ynnuf yaw ot etirw sdrow

answer
what a funny way to write words

badly
not done well
He played the piano badly.

badminton
a game like tennis that is played with rackets and a small object with feathers
We play badminton at the sports centre.

▽ **badminton**

racket

shuttlecock

bag
a container made of plastic, paper, cloth or leather
Put the vegetables into one bag.

baggy
loose, not tight
I like baggy sweaters.

bake (baking, baked)
to cook food in an oven
Bake the cake for 40 minutes.

balcony
an area outside a window where you can sit or stand
You can see the beach from the balcony.

bald
without hair
My dad is going bald.

ball
an object that you throw, hit or kick in games
Throw the ball in the air.

ballet
a type of dancing that tells a story with no words
Swan Lake is a very famous ballet.

◀ **ballet**

balloon
a rubber bag filled with air that is used as a decoration
We had balloons at the party.

•Puzzle time•

a. How many red balloons can you see?
b. How many blue balloons can you see?
c. How many purple balloons can you see?

a.3 b.3 c.2
answers

banana
a long, curved yellow fruit
I like bananas for breakfast.

▲ **bananas**

bang
a sudden loud noise
The door shut with a bang.

bank
1 a place to keep money
There is a bank in the town.
2 the land alongside a river
People sit on the bank and fish.

barn
a large farm building for keeping animals or crops
The cows are in the barn.

also look at farm

▲ **barn**

baseball
a game played by two teams who try to get points by hitting a ball and running around the four corners of a square
There are nine players on a baseball team.

basket
a container made of thin strips, to hold or carry things
Put the bread in the basket.

basketball
a game played by two teams who try to get points by throwing a ball through a round net
Basketball is a fast game.

▼ **basketball**

bat
1 a small animal that usually flies at night
Bats use sound to help them move around.
2 the stick used to hit a ball in games such as baseball and cricket
Baseball bats are round, cricket bats are flat.

▶ **bat**

bath
a long container that you fill with water and sit in to wash your body
I like sitting in a warm bath.

beach (beaches)
the land next to the sea
We had a picnic on the beach.

▲ **beach**

bean
the seed of a climbing plant that is eaten as food
I like baked beans on toast.

▶ **beans**

bear
a large, strong wild animal that is covered in fur
Bears have strong, sharp claws.

▲ **polar bear**

beard
hair that grows on a man's chin and cheeks
My Dad has a beard.

beautiful
very pleasant
Roses are beautiful flowers.

bed
a piece of furniture for sleeping on
There are two beds in my room.

bee
a yellow and black striped insect
Bees live in a nest called a hive.
also look at insect

▲ **bee**

begin (beginning, began)
to start
Begin at the top of the page.

behind
at the back of someone or something
She's hiding behind that fence.

bell
▼ **bell**
1 a hollow, metal object that makes a sound when hit
Press the bell for service.
2 a machine that makes a ringing sound
The bell rings at 3:15 p.m.

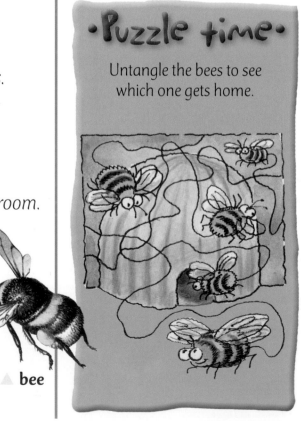

•Puzzle time•
Untangle the bees to see which one gets home.

below

in a lower place than
something else
The gym is on the floor below.

belt

a piece of clothing that you
wear around your waist
*Belts can be made of leather,
cloth or plastic.*

◀ **belt**

bench (benches)

a seat for two or more people
to sit on
Wait on the bench.

also look at chair

▲ **bench**

better (best)

*The new game is better than
the last one.*

also look at good

between

in a place or time that
separates two things or people
*She is sitting between her
brother and sister.*

beyond

after a place
It's just beyond the next hill.

bicycle (bike)

a machine with two wheels
that you sit on and move by
pushing on pedals to make
the wheels go round
*I'm asking for a new bicycle for
my birthday.*

saddle

wheel

chain

pedal

handlebar

spoke

▲ **bicycle**

•Puzzle time•

Can you unscramble the
names of these birds?

a. fupfin

b. eglae

c. eapccko

d. llguase

answers
a. puffin b. eagle
c. peacock d. seagull

big (bigger, biggest)

1 large, not small
The sweatshirt is too big.
2 important
Tomorrow is a big day.

bike

You can ride on a bike.

also look at bicycle

bird

an animal that has wings,
feathers and lays eggs
Most birds can fly.

▶ **bird**

birthday
the day of the year on which
a person is born
When is your birthday?

biscuit
a dry, thin cake that is
usually sweet
Would you like a biscuit?

bite (biting, bit, bitten)
to cut into something with
your teeth
Have a bite of the apple.

▲ **bite**

bitter
having a strong, sharp taste
such as coffee
Add more sugar, it tastes bitter.

blanket
a piece of material on a bed
that you use to keep warm
There's a blanket on the bed.

blind
not able to see
*Talking books are made for
blind people.*

blister
a raised piece of skin, filled
with liquid, caused by
burning or rubbing
I have a blister on my foot.

blizzard
a very heavy snow storm
*People shouldn't drive in
a blizzard.*

also look at weather

blood
the liquid that your heart
pumps through your body
Blood looks very red.

bloom (blooming, bloomed)
to open out into a flower
*There are flowers blooming all
over the garden.*

blow (blowing, blew)
to push air out of your
mouth.
It's fun to blow bubbles!

▽ **blow**

boat
a small ship
You get to the island by boat.

boat

Puzzle time
Find four different types of boat
in this word puzzle.

shipboatyachtferry
ship boat yacht ferry
answers

body (bodies)
1 the whole of a person
*Skin covers your
entire body.*
2 a dead person
*They covered
the body with
a blanket.*

bone
a hard, white
part under
the skin of a
person or animal
*Your body has
more than 200
bones*

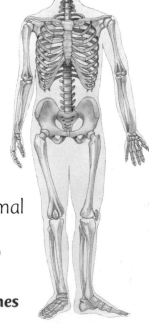

▷ **bones**

book

1 sheets of paper with writing on them joined together for reading
This is a book about spiders.
2 sheets of paper joined together for writing on
Write your name on the cover of your exercise book.

boot

1 a shoe that covers your foot and ankle
Wear your boots in the rain.
2 part of a car for carrying things
The bags are in the boot.

 boots

bored

not interested
I'm bored, let's play a game.

born

to start life
When were you born?

borrow (borrowing, borrowed)

to have something that belongs to another person and return it to them
You can borrow the books for two weeks.
also look at lend

bottle

a tall container for storing liquid
I have a water bottle on my bike.

▶ **bottles**

bottom

the lowest part of something
The number is at the bottom of the page.

bounce (bouncing, bounced)

1 to move back quickly after hitting or falling on something
Bounce on the trampoline.
2 to throw something against something so that it moves back quickly
Bounce the ball against the wall.

bow

1 a knot with loops
Tie a bow on top of the present.
2 a long, thin stick with string for shooting arrows or playing an instrument
You play the violin with a bow.

bow (bowing, bowed)

to bend your body or your head to show respect
People bowed to the king.

bowl

a deep, curved dish
You eat cereal out of a bowl.
also look at dish

box (boxes)

a container with four sides
Keep the crayons in a box.

boxing

the sport of fighting with closed hands
There is a boxing match on TV.

boy

a male child or a young man
There are two boys in their family.

bracelet

a piece of jewellery worn around the wrist
My bracelet has my name on it.
also look at jewellery

▲ **bracelet**

Braille

a type of printing that uses raised bumps
Blind people read by Braille.

Braille

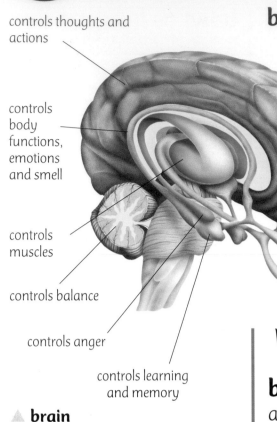

controls thoughts and actions

controls body functions, emotions and smell

controls muscles

controls balance

controls anger

controls learning and memory

▲ **brain**

brain

the part of your body inside your head that you use for thinking, feeling and moving
When you touch something hot, nerves send a message to your brain and you pull your hand away.

branch

the part of a tree that grows out from the trunk
Leaves, flowers and fruit grow on branches.

bread

a type of food made with flour, water and yeast
Have some bread and butter.

break (breaking, broke, broken)

to make something separate into two or more pieces
Carry the glass carefully so that you don't drop and break it.

breakfast

the first meal of the day
We had cereal for breakfast.

breeze

a light wind
There's a nice breeze blowing.

brick

a block of baked clay used for building
The wall is made from bricks.

bridge

a structure built to join two things, such as a road
There is a bridge over the river.

▲ **bridge**

bright

1 full of light
It's a bright, sunny day.
2 strong and easy to see
Wear bright colours when you go into the forest.
3 clever, intelligent
That's a bright idea.

brilliant

1 very bright and strong
The North Star is one of the most brilliant stars in the sky.
2 very good at doing something
She's a brilliant scientist.
3 very good or enjoyable
It's a brilliant game!

bring (bringing, brought)

to take something with you
Come over, and bring a friend.

broccoli

a green vegetable
Let's have broccoli with dinner.

broom

a brush with a handle
Sweep the floor with a broom.

brother

a boy or a man who has the same parents as another person
Nadia has two brothers.

also look at family

brush (brushes)
a tool with stiff hairs fastened to a handle that is used for sweeping, painting, cleaning or smoothing
Here is a brush to paint with.

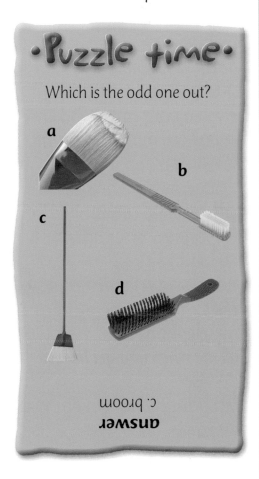

•Puzzle time•

Which is the odd one out?

a

b

c

d

answer
c. broom

bucket
a round, open container with a handle
Put the water in a bucket.

build (building, built)
to make something, such as a house, by putting pieces together
There are plans to build a new school next year.

building
a place with a roof and walls
The Taj Mahal is a building in India.

▲ **building**

bull
a male cow, elephant or whale
There's a bull running loose in that field.

burglar
a person who goes into buildings to steal things
A burglar stole the money.

burn (burning, burned, burnt)
1 to be alight or on fire
The candles are burning.
2 to hurt or destroy something with fire
The shed burnt down.

bus (buses)
a large vehicle that carries passengers
The bus stops at our road.

bush (bushes)
a plant like a small tree
Blackberries grow on bushes.

butter
a yellow food that is made from milk
Spread butter on the bread.

butterfly (butterflies)
an insect with large wings
Butterflies drink from flowers.
also look at cocoon

▶ **butterfly**

button
a small, round object that you push through a hole to fasten clothes
There are five buttons on my shirt.

buy (buying, bought)
to get something by paying money for it
Shall we buy some sweets?

Cc

cabbage
a large vegetable with thick, round leaves
Cabbages can be green, white or red.

▶ **cabbage**

cabin
1 a small house made of wood, usually in the country.
The cabin is halfway up the mountain.
2 the place where the passengers sit inside an aeroplane
The pilot walked back through the cabin.
3 a small room to sleep in on a ship
The cabin has two beds.

cactus (cactuses, cacti)
a plant that grows in hot, dry places that has needles instead of leaves
The needles on a cactus are sharp.

▶ **cactus**

café
a place that serves drinks and simple meals
That café has tables outside.

•Puzzle time•
Use the code to find out what they ordered at the café:

A	B	C	D	E	F	G	H	I	J
1	2	3	4	5	6	7	8	9	10

K	L	M	N	O	P	Q	R
11	12	13	14	15	16	17	18

S	T	U	V	W	X	Y	Z
19	20	21	22	23	24	25	26

16/9/26/26/1
19/1/12/1/4

answer
pizza and salad

cage
a room or box made of bars to keep animals or birds in
Hamsters and mice live in cages.

cake
a sweet food made of flour, sugar and eggs that is baked in an oven
Let's make a chocolate cake.

calendar
a special chart that shows the days, weeks and months of the year
We wrote everyone's birthday on the calendar in our classroom.

calf (calves)
▲ **calf**
1 a baby cow, elephant or whale
The calf is two days old.
2 the back part of your leg between your ankle and knee.
I've pulled a muscle in my calf.
also look at leg

call (calling, called)
1 to shout or say something in a loud voice
Dad calls us in for dinner at six o'clock.
2 to telephone
Call me when you get home.
3 to visit
The doctor calls when someone is very ill.
4 to give someone or something a name
They called the baby Luke.

▼ **camel**

camel
a large animal with one or two humps that can carry heavy loads
A camel can go without water for a long time.

camera

a piece of equipment used for taking photographs or filming
You get a digital camera free with this computer.

▲ **camera**

camp

a place where people stay in tents
The camp is over the hill.

camp (camping, camped)

to stay in a tent
Every summer the scouts camp in this field.

can

▶ **can**

a metal container
We collect drinks cans for charity.

can (could)

1 to be able to do something
Aziz can use the Internet.
2 to be allowed to do something
We can come to your party.
also look at may

candle

a stick of wax with a string through it that you burn for light
There are nine candles on her birthday cake.

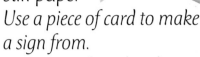

▲ **candle**

captain

1 someone who leads a team
Who is captain of the football team this year?
2 a person who is in charge of a ship or a plane
The captain says the flight will take two hours.

car

a machine on wheels that has an engine and that people can ride in
There is a car in the driveway.

▼ **car**

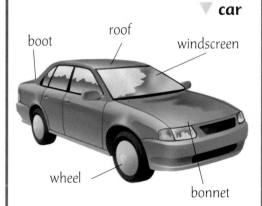

boot
roof
windscreen
wheel
bonnet

caravan

a small house on wheels that can be pulled behind a car
David and Katya have taken the caravan on holiday.

▶ **card**

card

1 thick, stiff paper
Use a piece of card to make a sign from.
2 a piece of card with words and a picture that you give or send someone
My brother gave me a birthday card to open.
3 a piece of stiff paper or plastic that you use to buy things or to identify yourself
I have a library card.
4 a piece of stiff paper with pictures and numbers that you use to play games
Give each player seven cards.

cardigan

a piece of clothing like a sweater with buttons down the front
Wear a cardigan if it's cold.

careful (carefully)

paying attention to what you are doing so that you don't make a mistake or have an accident
Be careful! That knife is sharp.

carpet

a thick cover for the floor
The carpet in my bedroom is green and blue.

carrot
a long,
orange
vegetable
that grows
under the ground
*Carrots are a very healthy food
to eat.*

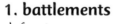
▲ **carrots**

carry (carrying, carried)
to move something from one
place to another
Can you help me carry this?

cassette
a plastic box with a tape
inside it for recording or
playing back sound or video
*Put the cassette into the
machine and press 'play'.*

castle
a large, strong building with
thick walls
*Castles were built to keep the
people inside safe from their
enemies.*

cat
a small, furry animal with
a long tail and sharp claws
*My cat likes to
climb trees.*

▶ **cat**

•Puzzle time•

The 't' in castle is silent, you
don't pronounce it when you
say the word.
Each of these words has
a silent letter – do you know
which ones are silent?

**calf   island   knee
knife   leopard**

Hint – you can look the words
up in this dictionary if you
don't know what they mean.

l**e**opard
ca**l**f **i**sland **k**nee **k**nife

answers

1. battlements
defensive areas on top
of castle walls
2. gatehouse
the towers and gates
which guard the
entrance to a castle
3. great hall
a big business room
inside a castle,
sometimes used for
feasting
4. portcullis
a heavy metal fence
that seals off the castle
gateway
5. tower
a tall building from
which enemies can
be seen

catch (catching, caught)
1 to get hold of something
Catch the ball!
2 to get an illness
*People often catch cold in the
winter.*
3 to get on a bus, train, plane
or ferry and go somewhere
*We usually catch
the bus to the
airport.*

Inside
a castle

caterpillar

an animal, like a worm
with legs, that turns
into a butterfly
or a moth
*Caterpillars
eat leaves.*

caterpillar

egg

chrysalis

butterfly

emerging
butterfly

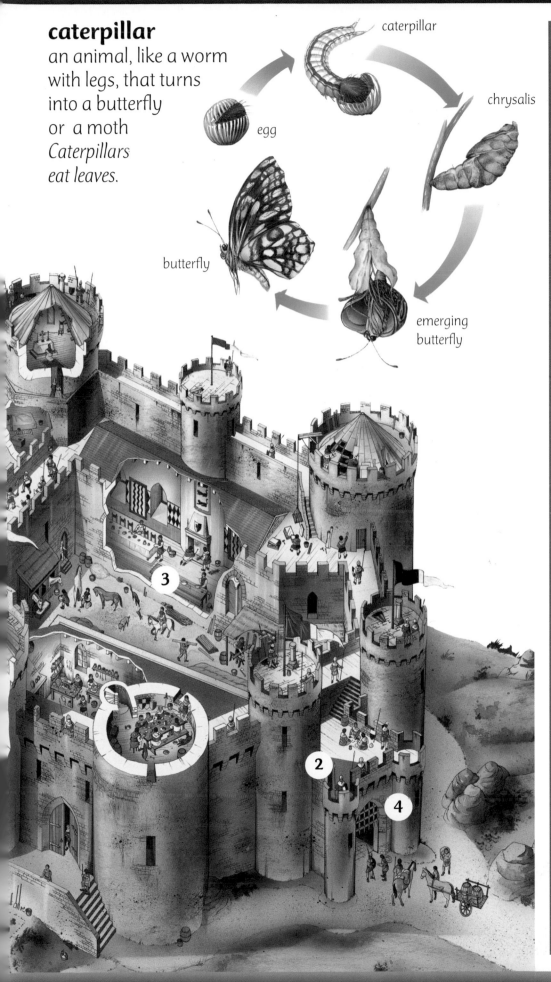

3

2

4

cave

a hole in a mountainside or
under the ground.
Caves are usually dark.

CD (CDs, compact disc)

a circular piece of plastic for
storing sound
Let's play a CD.

▶ CD

CD-ROM (CD-ROMs, compact disc read-only memory)

a circular piece of plastic for
storing information to be
used by a computer
*CD-ROMs hold lots of
information.*

celery

a vegetable that is often used
in salads
Celery is crunchy.

cereal

a breakfast food that is made
from plants such as wheat,
oats and rice.
Pour some milk on the cereal.

chair
a piece of furniture for sitting on
Pull your chair close to the desk.

◄ **chair**

chalk
a soft, white rock
We use different coloured chalk to draw the picture.

▼ **chameleon**

chameleon
a lizard that changes colour so its skin matches the things around it
Chameleons eat flies.

change (changing, changed)
1 to become different or to make something different
You haven't changed at all!
2 to put on different clothes
I'll be downstairs as soon as I've changed.

cheap (cheaper, cheapest)
not expensive
This watch is cheap but it is well-made.

cheese
a food that is made from milk
Cheese tastes very good.

cherry (cherries)
a small, round reddish fruit that has a stone in the centre
We'll have cherry pie.

▲ **cherries**

chest
1 the part of your body between your neck and your stomach
Place the belt across your chest.
2 a strong box with a top that locks
The chest was filled with gold!

chicken
a farm bird that is kept for eggs and meat
Chickens can't fly very far.

▲ **chicken**

child (children)
1 a young person
Entry is free for children.
2 someone's son or daughter
They love all their children.

chimney
an opening over a fire that takes smoke out through the roof of a building
The chimney is filled with soot.

▲ **chimneys**

chin
part of your face under your mouth
His beard hides his chin.
also look at face

chips
pieces of potato fried in oil
Do you like fish and chips?

chocolate
a sweet food made from cocoa beans
Would you like some chocolate?

Christmas
a Christian holiday
Where are you spending Christmas?
also look at holiday

church (churches)

the place where Christians meet to worship
The church is full of flowers.

cinema

a place you go to see films
Shall we go to the cinema?

circus (circuses)

a show with people and animals, held in a big tent
The circus is in town!

· Did you know? ·

Circuses are hundreds of years old. The first modern circus began in England in 1768, and involved horseback riding and live music. Today, modern circuses show breathtaking tricks and stunts.

city (cities)

a large town
It is a big, busy city.   ▼ **city**

clap (clapping, clapped)

to make a loud sound by hitting the palms of your hands together
The actors bowed and we clapped louder.

class (classes)

1 a group of people who learn together
We're in the same class.
2 a group of things or animals that are the same
People belong to the class of animals called mammals.

claw

a sharp, hard part of an animal's foot
Cats have sharp claws.

clean (cleaning, cleaned)

to make something tidy, to take dirt away
Clean your room!

clean

not dirty
The car is clean and shiny.

clear

1 easy to understand, hear or read
The instructions are clear.
2 easy to see through
You can see the fish swimming in the clear water.

clever

able to learn or understand things quickly
Well done – you're very clever.

◄ **circus**

cliff

the side of a rock or mountain
The road runs along a cliff.

▲ cliff

climb (climbing, climbed)

to move upwards
She climbed to the top.

▶ climb

clock

a machine that tells the time
The clock said 5:55 a.m.

▲ clock

close (closing, closed)

to shut
Close the window, I'm cold.

close

near
The hotel is close to the beach.

cloth

1 a soft material
The chair is covered in cloth.
2 a piece of cloth for a special purpose
Clean the window with a cloth.

clothes

things that people wear
Shirts, jeans and skirts are all clothes.

cloud

a white or grey object in the sky that is made of tiny drops of water
It's a beautiful day, just a few small clouds.

clown

someone who makes people laugh
Harry is our class clown.

▶ clown

coast

the land next to the sea
The village is on the coast.

coat

a piece of clothing you wear over your clothes to stay warm or keep the rain off
This is a warm coat.

coconut

the nut of the palm tree
Coconuts give delicious juice.

cocoon

the bag around an insect that protects it while it is growing
The cocoon broke open and a butterfly flew out.
also look at butterfly and caterpillar

◀ cocoon

coffee

the brown beans of a plant, or a hot drink made from them
Do you want coffee or tea?

coin

a piece of money that is made of metal
They keep coins from their holidays.

cold

not warm or hot
Brrr — this water is very cold.

collect (collecting, collected)
to put things together in one place
Some people collect coins, others collect stamps.

colour
blue, green, red and yellow
What colour is your jacket?

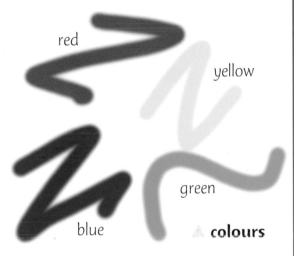
red
yellow
green
blue
▲ **colours**

colour (colouring, coloured)
to make something a colour with paint, crayons or ink
We coloured the picture in.

comb
an object with teeth for making your hair tidy
You shouldn't let anyone use your comb.

◀ **comb**

comic
a magazine with pictures that tell a story
Comics are often funny.

compass
an object that shows you what direction you are travelling in
If you can read a compass, you can find the treasure!

▲ **compass**

competition
a test to see who is best at something
There was a singing competition on the radio.

complain (complaining, complained)
to say that something is wrong and you are not happy about it
He complained to the waiter.

computer
a machine for storing information and doing jobs such as sums and writing letters
You can play games on computers.
▲ **computer**

confused
a feeling of not being sure
I was confused by the question.

container
something that holds something else inside it
Jars, tins and boxes are all different kinds of containers.

cook (cooking, cooked)
to make food hot so that it can be eaten
Ahmed is cooking dinner for us.

cool
a little bit cold
The sun is hot but there is a cool breeze.

copy (copying, copied)
to do something the same as something else
Copy the words on the board.

corn
1 a plant with large, yellow seeds
This corn is delicious.
2 the seeds of plants such as wheat and oats
Many farmers grow different types of corn every year.

▲ **corn**

cough (coughing, coughed)
to force air from your throat
*She's still coughing, give her
a drink of water.*

count (counting, counted)
to find out how many
*Count the children in the
playground.*

country (countries)
1 a place with its own
government
Which country do you live in?
2 away from cities and
towns.
*We live in a village in the
country.*

cousin
the child of your aunt
or uncle
Charlie is my cousin.
also look at family

cow (cows, cattle)
a large, female farm animal
that gives milk
Cows eat grass.

cowboy
a man who rides a horse and
takes care of cattle
*The cowboy tried to
ride the horse.*

▲ **cowboy**

crab
a sea animal that moves
sideways
and has
big claws
*Crabs
are good
to eat.*

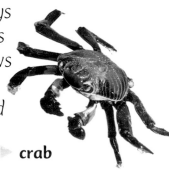
▶ **crab**

crack
where something is broken
There's a crack in this mug.

crack (cracking, cracked)
to break something so that
a line appears on it
Just crack the shell.

crash (crashing, crashed)
1 to have an accident
The car crashed into a tree.
2 to make a loud noise
Hear the thunder crash!

crawl (crawling, crawled)
to move around on your
hands and knees
The baby is crawling.

crayon
a coloured wax stick
Can I use your crayons?

creep (creeping, crept)
to move so that no one sees or
hears you
Oh! Don't creep up on me!

crisps
fried, thin slices of potato
I love eating crisps.

crocodile
a large animal with a long
body, short legs and big teeth
that lives in rivers and lakes
Crocodiles live in hot countries.

▼ **crocodile**

crooked

not straight
The fence is very crooked.

crop

plants that are grown to be
eaten or used to make things
*The weather is very important
to farmers who grow crops.*

cross

two lines that go over
each other
*There is a cross on the map
where the treasure is hidden.*

cross (crossing, crossed)

to go from one side of
something to the other
Cross the road carefully.

crown

▼ **crown**

a metal circle
that kings and
queens wear on
their heads
*The queen and king are both
wearing gold crowns.*

cruel

not kind
He's a cruel king.

crumb

A small piece of something
such as bread or cake
There are only crumbs left.

cry (crying, cried)

1 to make tears from your
eyes, usually because you
feel sad or are hurt
*Sometimes you feel better after
you cry.*
2 to shout
'Help! Help!' they cried.

▶ **cry**

cucumber

a long, thin green vegetable
that is used in salads
*I'd like a cucumber and tomato
salad.*

cuddle (cuddling, cuddled)

to hold someone in your
arms to show you care
*Chloe cuddled her best friend
to cheer her up.*

◀ **cuddle**

cup

a container with a handle for
drinking from
*Put a teabag in the cup, then
add water.*

cupboard

a piece of furniture for storing
things
*Please dry the dishes and put
them in the cupboard.*

curious

wanting to know or find out
about something
Cats are very curious.

curl

something like hair or ribbon
that is curved at the end
She has beautiful curls.

◀ **curls**

curtain

cloth that hangs across or
over a window
Pull the curtains at night.

cushion

a bag with soft material
inside for sitting or lying on
Put a cushion under your head.

cut (cutting, cut)

to remove something with
a knife or scissors.
I'm going to get my hair cut.

Dd

daisy (daisies)
a flower with white petals and a yellow centre
You can make a chain of daisies.

▼ **daisies**

dance (dancing, danced)
to move your body to music
This music is good to dance to.

dangerous
not safe
Playing with matches is dangerous.

dark
not light
We stay out and play until it gets dark.

daughter
a female child
Her daughter's name is Amy.

·Puzzle time·
Can you match the pictures to the time of day?

a. eat breakfast **b.** play

c. do homework **d.** clean teeth

a. morning b. afternoon
c. evening d. morning/night
answers

day
1 a 24-hour period
We're staying for three days.
2 from the time the sun rises until it sets
Bats do not fly during the day.

dead
not alive
This plant looks dead.

deaf
not able to hear
Many deaf people can read lips.

dear
1 a word to start a letter
Dear Aran, How are you?
2 much cared about
She's a very dear friend.
3 expensive
The dress is too dear.

deep
a long way from the top to the bottom, or from the front to the back
I'm not afraid to swim in the deep end of the pool.

deer (deer)
an animal that lives in forests
Deer are gentle animals.

▲ **deer**

delicious
tasting very good
This ice cream is delicious.

delighted
very happy
I'm delighted with my new bike.

dentist

a person who looks after people's teeth
I go to the dentist twice a year.

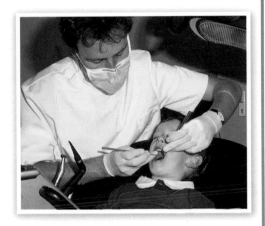

▲ **dentist**

desert

a place where there is very little or no rain
Most deserts are hot.

▲ **desert**

desk

a piece of furniture that you sit at to read, write or use a computer
There's a lamp on my desk.

dessert

sweet food that you eat at the end of a meal
What's for dessert?

▲ **dessert**

detective

a person who finds out information about a crime or another person
Some police officers are detectives.

diary

a book with the days of the year in it that you use to write down what you plan to do or what you have done
I write in my diary every week.

die (dice)

a cube with spots on each side that is used for playing games
It's your turn — throw the dice.

▲ **dice**

die (dying, died)

to stop living
Water the plant before it dies.

different

not the same
These two sweets look the same but they taste different.

difficult

not easy
I hope the spelling test isn't too difficult.

dig (digging, dug)

to make a hole in earth or to move it.
Big machines can dig faster than we can.

▲ **dig**

digital

1 showing information using numbers that can change
This is a digital watch.
2 storing information using only zero and one
Most music is digitally recorded these days.

dining room

the room in which you eat your meals.
The dining room is next to the kitchen in our house.
also look at house

dinner

the main evening meal
What's for dinner?

dinosaur

an animal that became extinct 65 million years ago
Tyrannosaurus Rex is one type of dinosaur.

also look at fossil

• Did you know? •

The first record of dinosaur bones being found was less than 200 years ago. The bones were found in 1818 by Solomon Ellsworth, Jr., while he was digging a well at his home in Windsor, Connecticut, U.S.A.

dirty

not clean, messy
We put dirty clothes in the washing basket.

disabled

a disabled person cannot use part of their body
This parking space is for disabled drivers only.

disappear (disappearing, disappeared)

to go out of sight or become impossible to find
The sun disappeared behind a cloud.

disco

a place or a party where people dance
There's a disco on Saturday.

discover (discovering, discovered)

to find or understand something for the first time
Alexander Fleming discovered penicillin, a type of medicine.

disease

a serious illness
Flu is a disease.

disguise

something that you wear to hide who you really are
Part of his disguise is a false beard.

▼ disguise

dish (dishes)

something like a bowl or plate, that is for serving food
Please help me wash the dishes.

Stegosaurus

Stenonychosaurus

Quetzalcoatus

Diplodocus

Ankylosaurus

Pteradactyl

Seismosaurus

▲ dinosaurs

a b c d e f g h i j k l m

disk
a piece of plastic for storing computer information
Save the file on a disk.

dive (diving, dived)
to go into water head-first
I'm learning to dive.

▲ dive

Diwali
an important Hindu festival
also look at holiday

dizzy
the feeling that things are turning around you or that you are going to fall
That ride makes me dizzy.

doctor
a person who looks after sick people or helps stop people from being ill
Doctors work very hard.

▼ doctor

document
1 papers that contain official information
There are important old documents on display at the museum.
2 a piece of work that is saved in a file on a computer
You can attach a document to an email.

dog
an animal that people keep as a pet
Our dog is a sheep dog.

doll
a toy that looks like a person
Let's play with our dolls.

dolphin
a large animal that lives in the sea
There are places where you can swim with dolphins.

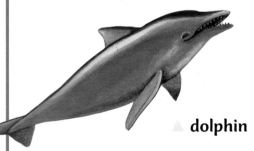

▲ dolphin

domino (dominoes)
a piece of black wood or plastic with white spots that is used to play games
Playing dominoes is good for your maths!

▼ donkey

donkey
an animal that looks like a small horse with big ears
There are donkeys in that field.

door
something that you open and close to go into or out of a room, house or car
Can you open the door for me?

down
1 towards a lower place
Get down off the ladder.
2 at a lower rate or speed
Prices are coming down.

dragon
an imaginary animal like a big lizard that breathes fire
The story is about a princess trapped in a dragon's cave.
also look at fairy tale

▶ dragon

dramatic
surprising or exciting
It's dramatic news.

draw (drawing, drew, drawn)
to make
a picture
*You can
draw very
well.*

▶ **draw**

drawer
part of a piece of furniture
that slides in and out that is
used for storing things
Put the clothes in the drawer.

dream (dreaming, dreamt or dreamed)
1 to think about or see things
in your sleep
*Last night I dreamed that I
could fly.*
2 to hope for something
We dream of being famous.

dress (dressing, dressed)
to put clothes on
Get dressed, we're ready to go.

dress (dresses)
a piece of clothing for girls
or women that has a top
and skirt
That's a beautiful dress.

drink
liquid food
*Coffee, tea, juice and milk are
different kinds of drinks.*

▲ **drink**

drink (drinking, drank, drunk)
to take liquid into your mouth
and swallow it
Drink lots of water.

drive (driving, drove, driven)
to control a vehicle, like a car
My oldest brother can drive.

drop (dropping, dropped)
to fall or to let something fall
Don't drop that vase.

drum
a musical
instrument
that you hit with a
stick or your hand
He plays the drums.
also look at music

▲ **drum**

•Puzzle time•
How many things begin with
'd' in this picture?

dry
not wet
The washing is nearly dry.

duck
a bird with webbed feet that
lives near water
We feed bread to the ducks.

▼ **duck**

dustbin
a big container for storing
rubbish
*The dustbins are emptied
on Tuesdays.*

DVD (digital versatile disk)
a circular piece of
plastic used for
storing and playing
music and films
Is the film on DVD?

Ee

eagle
a bird that hunts for its food
An eagle has sharp claws and a beak.

▶ eagle

ear
the part of your body that you use to hear
My ears feel cold.

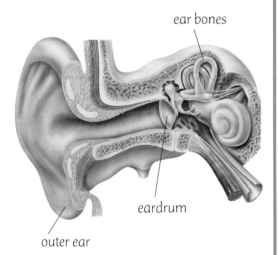

ear bones

eardrum

outer ear

▲ ear

early
before the normal time
I wake up early in the summer.

earn (earning, earned)
to get money for work
I earn extra pocket money for washing the car.

earring
a piece of jewellery that is worn on the ear
I wore my new earrings to the party.

▲ earrings

Earth (earth)
1 the planet we live on
Earth travels around the Sun.
2 soil
Sprinkle earth over the seeds.

▶ Earth

earthquake
a strong shaking of the earth
Earthquakes can cause serious damage to buildings.

Easter
a Christian holiday
also look at holiday

▲ Easter eggs

·Puzzle time·
How many Easter eggs can you find?

easy
not difficult
This book is easy to read.

eat (eating, ate, eaten)
to take food into your mouth and swallow it
I'm so hungry I could eat a horse!

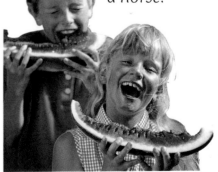

▲ eating

echo (echoes)
a sound that bounces off something and can be heard again
There is a strong echo when you shout into the cave.

egg
1 an oval object with a shell that some animals lay, from which their babies hatch
There are four eggs in the nest.
2 an egg used as food
I can make fried eggs.

▷ **eggs**

elbow
where your arm bends
Ouch, I bumped my elbow.

electricity
power that is used to make lights and machines work
Lightning is a giant spark of electricity.

elephant
a large, wild animal with a long nose called a trunk
A baby elephant is called a calf.

▲ **elephant**

email
messages sent by computer
I email all my friends.

empty
with nothing inside
The box is empty.

end
to finish or stop
The film ends at 6:30 p.m.

enemy (enemies)
someone who does not like you, or wants to hurt you
We are enemies, not friends.

energy
strength or power
We're trying to save energy.

engine
1 a machine that makes something work
Engines are in the front of cars.
2 The part of a train that pulls the other carriages
The steam engine is very noisy.

enjoy (enjoying, enjoyed)
to like to do something
I enjoy playing tennis.

enormous
very, very big
Whales are enormous animals.

enough
as much as you need
There is enough for everyone.

enter (entering, entered)
1 to go into a place
The king entered the hall.
2 to put information into a computer
The names and addresses are entered in a file.

entrance
the way into a place
The entrance to the cave was very dark.

▽ **engine**

engine

a b c d **e** f g h i j k l m

envelope

a paper cover for letters and cards
Put a stamp on the envelope.

▲ **envelopes**

environment

everything around us, such as land, air or water
They live in a hot environment.

equal

the same as something else in number, size or amount
One kilogram is equal to 1,000 grams.

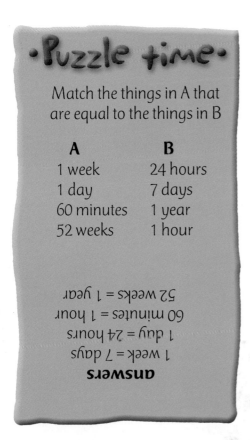

•Puzzle time•

Match the things in A that are equal to the things in B

A	B
1 week	24 hours
1 day	7 days
60 minutes	1 year
52 weeks	1 hour

answers
1 week = 7 days
1 day = 24 hours
60 minutes = 1 hour
52 weeks = 1 year

equipment

things that are used to do something like work or sport
Our school has lots of new computer equipment.

escalator

a staircase that moves
We went up the escalator.

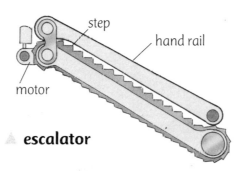
step
hand rail
motor
▲ **escalator**

escape (escaping, escaped)

to leave a place that is dangerous or unpleasant
They escaped from the prison.

evening

the time of day between afternoon and night time
It starts to get dark in the evening.

▲ **evening**

excellent

very good
This is an excellent song.

excited

happy and interested in something
I am excited about tomorrow.

▼ **excited**

excuse

a reason you give for something that you have said or done
Her excuse for being late is that she overslept.

exercise

movements that you make to stay fit and healthy
Exercise keeps you healthy.

▼ **exercise**

exhibition

a show where people can look at things like paintings
There is an exhibition of our artwork at school.

exit

the way to leave a place
There is a light over the exit.

expensive

costing a lot
Jewellery can be very expensive to buy.

explain (explaining, explained)

to say what something means or why it has happened
Our teacher explained how the equipment worked.

explanation

what something means or why it happened
There is a good explanation for the accident.

explode

(exploding, exploded)
to suddenly burst or blow up into small pieces
The fireworks exploded in the night sky.

explore (exploring, explored)

to look around a new place
We explored the cave.

▲ explore

explosion

the noise, smoke, and sometimes flames, that are made when something blows up into pieces
The explosion filled the air with clouds of smoke.

• Did you know? •

Your eyes measure only 2.5 centimetres across, but they can see things as far away as a star in space, and objects as tiny as a grain of sand.

▶ **parts of the eye**

extinct

no longer existing
The dodo is an extinct bird.

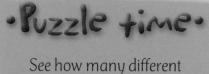
▼ extinct

dodo

•Puzzle time•

See how many different words you can make from

extinct

you should be able to make at least seven.

extra

more than is necessary
People are extra nice to you on your birthday.

eye

the part of the body that animals use to see
What colour are your eyes?

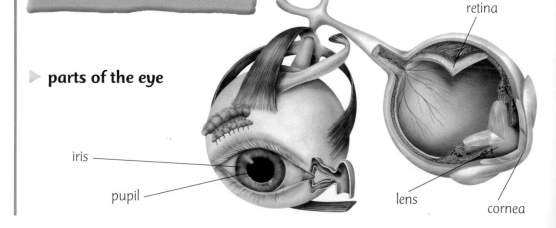

retina

iris

pupil

lens

cornea

Ff

face
the front part of your head
Your eyes, nose and mouth are on your face.

▶ **face**

factory
a place where things are made in large numbers by machines and people
Hundreds of people work at the car factory.

faint
1 not strong or easy to hear, see or smell
There is a faint smell of smoke.
2 feeling weak and light-headed
I am so hungry I feel faint.

fair
1 good and reasonable
Their decision is fair.
2 light coloured
He has fair hair and blue eyes.
3 fine, pleasant
If the weather is fair, we'll go to the beach.

fairy (fairies)
a magical person with wings
Tinkerbell is the name of the fairy in Peter Pan.

▼ **fairy**

fairy tale
a story for children about magical things
Some fairy tales are very old.

▲ **fairy tale**

fake
not real
Her coat is fake fur.

fall (falling, fell, fallen)
to drop downwards
My little brother is learning to walk but he keeps falling over.

false
not true, correct or real
He gave a false name.

family (families)
a group of people who are related to each other
There are nine people in their family.

▼ **family**

famous
well-known
He's a famous football player.

fan
▼ **fan**
1 an object that you hold in your hand and move, or a machine that moves the air to make it cooler
Sit in front of the fan and relax.
2 someone who likes a particular thing or person very much
My uncle is a Beatles fan.

far (faraway)
not near, a distance away
*I love getting letters from
faraway places.*

farm
a place where people grow
crops and raise animals
Cows are kept on dairy farms.

▲ **farm**

fast
quick, not slow
Racing cars are very fast.

fat
1 weighing more than is
good or normal
*If you eat too many sweets,
you might get fat.*
2 thick, big or wide
*Our teacher reads to us
from a big, fat book.*

father
a male parent
*My father reads to
me at night.*

favourite
liked the best
Blue is my favourite colour.

fax (faxes)
1 a document sent by a fax
There's a fax for you.
2 a machine that you use to
send documents down a
telephone line
Use the fax to send a message.

fear (fearing, feared)
to have the feeling that
something bad is going to
happen or has happened
There is nothing to fear!

feast
a large, special meal to
celebrate something
*Christmas dinner is a feast
at our house.*

feather
one of the soft, light things
that cover a bird's body
*Peacock feathers are
beautiful colours.*

◄ **feather**

feed (feeding, fed)
to give food to a
person or an animal
*It's fun to feed
the chickens.*

▼ **feed**

feel (feeling, felt)
1 to have an emotion
I feel happy to be home.
2 to touch or be touched by
something
This sweater feels rough.

female
a woman, girl or animal that
can have babies when adult
Female sheep are called ewes.

fence

a wall made of wood or wire
There are plants growing up our garden fence.

fence

ferry (ferries)

a kind of ship
The ferry leaves at 8:00 a.m.

ferry

few

1 not many
There are very few tickets left.
2 a small number
There are a few new messages.

field

a piece of land for growing crops, raising animals or playing sports
There is a bull in that field.

fierce

angry and strong, or violent
Guard dogs can be very fierce.

fierce

fight

when two or more people try to hurt each other
There is a fight outside.

file

1 information on a computer
Move your files to a new folder.
2 information about a person or subject kept for a reason
The doctor has files on all of the patients.

figure

1 a written number
Write all the figures down.
2 a person's shape
She saw the figure of a woman in the shadows.

fill (filling, filled)

to put things into something until it is full
Fill the vase with clean water for the flowers.

film

1 thin plastic that you put into a camera to take photographs
Digital cameras don't use film.
2 a movie
We saw the film at the cinema.

film

find (finding, found)

to see or get something that you are looking for
Can you find the answer?

·Puzzle time·
What is the missing letter?

fin_sh   f_ght
f_eld   f_erce

answers
finish fight field fierce

fine

1 very thin or in small pieces
The beach is covered with fine, white sand.
2 very good
They are fine singers.

finger

one of the five long parts on your hand
Your thumb is a finger.

▶ **fingers**

finish

(finishing, finished)
to end
Put your pencil down when you have finished.

fire

something that burns, giving out heat and flames
We had a fire in the fireplace.

fire engine

a truck used to put out fires
Fire engines have flashing lights.

firework

small objects that explode into bright colours in the sky
The fireworks start after dark.

▼ **fireworks**

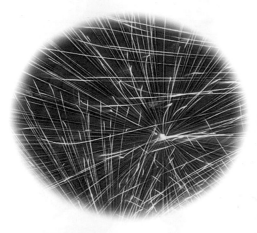

fish

an animal that lives underwater, has fins and breathes through gills
There are seven fish in the tank.

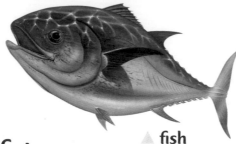

▲ **fish**

fist

a closed hand
Can you guess which fist the coin is in?

fit

to look and feel healthy
I feel very fit.

fix **(fixing, fixed)**

1 to mend, to repair
Dad is fixing the tractor.
2 to stick or attach
Fix the picture to the board.

▼ **fix**

flag

a piece of cloth that is used as a signal, or the sign of a country.
The stars and stripes are on the flag of the United States of America.

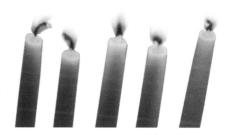

◀ **flag**

flame

the burning gas from a fire or bright light from a candle
The flames were very bright.

▲ **flames**

flash

a bright burst of light
You can see the lightning flash.

flat

1 a room or rooms in a bigger building
My uncle lives in a flat.
2 not bumpy or hilly, smooth
Put the paper flat on the table.

flavour

the taste of something
Strawberry, chocolate and vanilla are flavours of ice cream

•Puzzle time•

What flavours are the ice creams?
What is the missing letter?

a v_nill_

b chocol_te

c str_wberry

d ban_n_

answers
a vanilla **b** chocolate
c strawberry **d** banana

flight

a journey in a plane
The flight from New York to London takes about five hours.

float (floating, floated)

to stay on top of water or another liquid, not to sink
It is easier to float if you relax.

▲ float

flood

a lot of water in a place that is usually dry
There were heavy rains and then a flood.

floor

the part of a building you stand on
Everyone is sitting on the floor.

flower

the part of a plant that makes the seeds or fruit
Roses, pansies, daffodils and daisies are all flowers.

petal stem stamen

▲ flower

fly (flying, flew)

1 to move through the air
We flew at night.
2 a small insect
The fly was buzzing around.

▼ fly

fog

mist or cloud
You can't see very far in fog.

▲ fog

fold (folding, folded)

to turn or bend something over on itself
Fold your clothes.

follow (following, followed)

to move after or behind someone or something
Follow me!

food

something that people or animals eat
This food tastes delicious.

•Puzzle time•

How many different foods can you find in the word puzzle?

**ricefruitvegetablesmeat
chickensoupsandwich
saladbread**

answer
nine

foolish
silly
It is a foolish idea.

foot (feet)
the part of your body at the end of your leg that you stand and walk on
My father has very big feet.

football
a game that is played by two teams who try to kick a ball into a net to score goals
We play football every day.

forget (forgetting, forgotten)
to not remember something
Don't forget your homework.

fork
1 something with a handle and two or more points that is used for eating
The fork goes to the left of the plate.
2 a tool used for digging.
Turn the soil with a fork.
3 the place in a road or river that divides in two
There is a fork in the road.

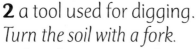
▼ fork

forwards
towards the front
Take two steps forwards.

fossil
the print of an animal or plant that lived long ago
Fossils show us what life was like millions of years ago.

▲ fossil

fountain
a jet of water that is pushed up into the air
There is a fountain in the city centre.

▲ fountain

▼ fox

fox (foxes)
a wild animal that looks like a dog with a bushy tail
Baby foxes are called cubs.

fraction
a part of something
A half, a third and a quarter are fractions.

$$\frac{1}{4} = a \; quarter$$

▲ fraction

frame
the thing that fits around a door, window or picture
Frames can be wood or metal.

freckle
a small, reddish-brown spot on a person's skin
Misha has freckles on her face.

free
1 not controlled
Wednesday afternoon is free time at our school.
2 not costing anything
The Internet is free for schools until 6:30 p.m.

freeze (freezing, froze, frozen)

to turn to ice because the temperature is very cold
Water freezes at 0°C.

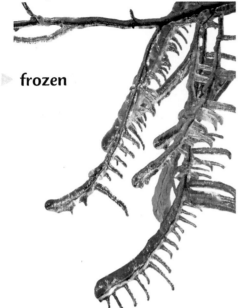

▷ **frozen**

fresh

1 just picked, grown or made
Fresh fruits and vegetables are healthy foods.
2 clean and pure
Go out and get some fresh air.

friend

a person you know and like
Good friends are very special.

▽ **friends**

friendly

kind and easy to get on with
We have very friendly neighbours.

frighten (frightening, frightened)

to scare, to make afraid
Storms may frighten animals.

frog

an animal with long legs that lives on land and in water
There are frogs in the pond.

▲ **frog**

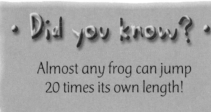
· Did you know? ·

Almost any frog can jump 20 times its own length!

front

the part of something that is the most forward
I sit at the front of the class.

frost

white, icy powder that forms when it is very cold outside
The trees are covered in frost.

▲ **frost**

frown (frowning, frowned)

to have a sad, angry or worried look on your face
Try not to frown.

fruit

the part of a plant that has seeds such as an apple, peach or grape
There is fruit in this yoghurt.

▷ **fruit**

fry (frying, fried)
to cook something using oil
Fry the fish until it is cooked.

▲ fry

full
containing as much as possible
Is the tank full yet?

fun
enjoyable
This website is really fun.

funny
making you laugh
The puppy is very funny.

▲ funny

fur (furry)
soft, thick hair on the skin of an animal
The kitten has soft, fluffy fur.

▼ furry

furniture
things in a room such as chairs, tables, beds and desks
We have new furniture in the dining room.

future
the time after now
In the future, we will have computers in our clothes.

fuzzy
1 not clear
These pictures are fuzzy.
2 curly and soft
My sister has fuzzy hair.

▼ furniture

chair

table

wardrobe

bed

Gg

gallop (galloping, galloped)
how animals such as horses or zebras run
See the zebras gallop away.

▲ galloping

game
an activity that has rules
Let's play a board game.

garage
1 a place to keep a car
The garage is next to the house.
2 a place where cars are repaired
The car is at the garage.

•Puzzle time•
See how many different words you can make from

garage

you should be able to make at least seven.

garden
land where flowers and plants can be grown
The garden is full of flowers.

▲ garden

gate
a door in a fence or wall
There is a gate between our garden and our neighbour's.

gentle
1 kind and careful not to hurt or disturb people or things
She is gentle with the animals.
2 not loud or strong
There is a gentle breeze blowing.

▽ gentle

geography
the study of countries
I like geography because we read about people and places.

ghost
a dead person's spirit
Do you believe in ghosts?

▶ ghost

giant
an imaginary person who is very big
The story is about a giant.
also look at fairy tale

▲ giant

gift
something given to someone, a present
That's a lovely gift, thank you.

giraffe
a very tall wild animal
with a long neck
*Giraffes live
in Africa.*

◄ **giraffe**

girl
a female child
*There are fifteen
girls in our class.*

► **girl**

give (gave, given)
1 to let someone have
something
We gave our teacher a present.
2 to pass something to
someone
Give this cup to your sister.

glad
happy about something
We're so glad you could come.

glass
1 hard, clear material that is
used to make windows,
bottles and mirrors
*The fish live in a
glass bowl.*
2 a container for
drinking from
*I have a glass of
water next to my
bed.*

► **glass**

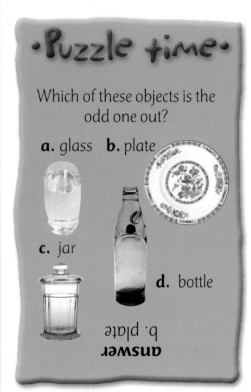

•Puzzle time•

Which of these objects is the
odd one out?

a. glass   **b.** plate

c. jar

d. bottle

answer
b. plate

glasses
two pieces of glass or plastic
that you wear to protect your
eyes or to see better
I wear glasses for reading.

▼ **glasses**

gloomy
1 dark
It's a gloomy day.
2 sad
Don't look so gloomy, smile!

glove
a piece of clothing to wear on
your hands
Where are your gloves?

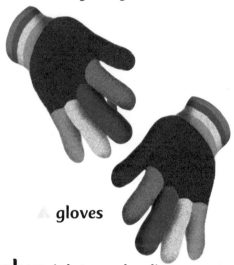

▲ **gloves**

glue (gluing, glued)
to stick things together
Glue the corners first.

goal
1 the posts in a game like
football or hockey where the
player tries to put the ball
*The goalkeeper is a very
important player.*
2 the point given to a team
when it gets the ball inside
the goal
*That's another goal for our
team.*
3 something you hope to do
My goal is to be a teacher.

goat

an animal like a sheep, usually with horns
Goats will eat almost anything.

goat

gold

1 a valuable, yellow metal
The ring is made of gold.
2 the colour of this metal
The present is wrapped up in gold paper.

gold

good (better, best)

1 of high quality
Our school is very good.
2 pleasant
I'm having a good time.
3 well-behaved
They are really good children.

good-bye (bye)

something you say when you are leaving someone
Good-bye and good luck!

goose (geese)

an animal like a big duck
There are geese on the farm.

geese

goosebumps

little bumps on your skin that appear when you are cold or frightened
The spooky story gave me goosebumps.

gorilla

the biggest kind of ape
She studies gorillas.

gorilla

• Did you know? •
Gorillas were relatively unknown until the mid 1800s. The first gorilla was shown in a zoo in the United States, in 1911.

grandparents
(grandfather, grandmother)

the parents of your mother or father
Our grandparents live with us.

▲ grandparents

grape

a small, round, juicy fruit that grows in bunches
Grapes are red, green or purple.

grapes

grass

a green plant with thin leaves that grows over the ground
My brother is cutting the grass.

gravity

the force that pulls things towards Earth and other planets
Gravity is what makes things fall to the ground.

harbour
a safe place for ships and boats near land
The fishing boats leave the harbour early in the morning.

▲ harbour

hard
1 not soft
This bed is very hard.
2 difficult, not easy
The questions are very hard.

hat
a piece of clothing that you wear on your head
You must wear a hat in the sun.

▲ hat

hate (hating, hated)
to strongly dislike something or someone
My cat hates going to the vet.

head
1 the part of your body above your neck
Put your hands on your head.
2 a person who is the leader
The head of the school is in charge.

healthy
well and strong
Our new baby is a healthy girl.

hear (hearing, heard)
1 to get sounds using your ears
Can you hear the rain?
2 to get news or be told something
I hear you're moving away.

heart
1 the part of your body that pumps your blood
Your heart beats faster when you run.
2 the main part of something
It's in the heart of the city.
3 a shape that means love
Valentine cards are decorated with hearts.

also look at shapes

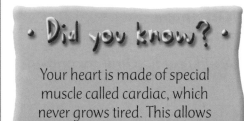

Did you know?

Your heart is made of special muscle called cardiac, which never grows tired. This allows your heart to beat an amazing 30 million times every year!

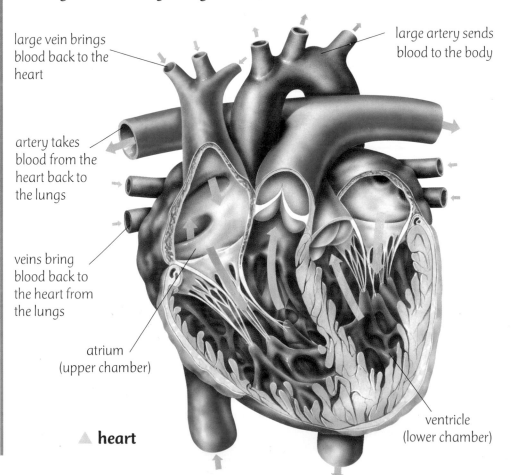

large vein brings blood back to the heart

large artery sends blood to the body

artery takes blood from the heart back to the lungs

veins bring blood back to the heart from the lungs

atrium (upper chamber)

ventricle (lower chamber)

▲ heart

heat (heating, heated)
to make something warm
Heat the soup but don't boil it.

heavy
weighing a lot
These books are really heavy.

hedgehog
a small, wild animal with
sharp hairs on its back
Hedgehogs like milk.

heel
1 the back part of
your foot
*Your heel is under
your ankle.*
2 The part of a
shoe that is under
your heel.
*Mum's shoes have
high heels.*

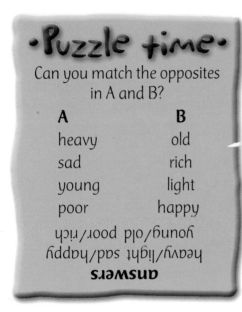
heel
▲ **heel**

height
how tall something is
*What is your height in
centimetres?*

helicopter
an aircraft with blades on top
that spin and make it fly
*Helicopters can land in smaller
spaces than planes.*

▼ **helicopter**

hello
what you say when you see
or meet someone, or when
you answer the telephone
Hello! How are you?

helmet
a hat that protects your head
*Always wear a helmet when you
ride your bike.*

▲ **helmet**

help (helping, helped)
to make it easier for someone
to do something
Let me help you lift that

hen
a female chicken
Hens lay eggs.

here
in this place
I like it here.

hibernate (hibernating,
hibernated)
to sleep during cold weather
*Some animals hibernate
in winter.*

hide (hiding, hid, hidden)
to put yourself or something
out of sight
Hide the presents, she's coming.

high

1 a long way from the bottom to the top
Mount Everest is the highest mountain on Earth.
2 a long way above
The plane is high above us.

▼ **high**

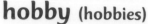

· Did you know? ·
Mount Everest is the highest point on Earth at 8,848 metres – that's 27 times higher than the Eiffel Tower in Paris, France!

hill
ground that is raised
Run down the hill.

▼ **hills**

hippopotamus (hippopotamuses, hippopotami)
a large animal that lives near rivers and lakes in Africa
Hippopotamuses leave the water at night to eat grass.

▲ **hippopotamuses**

history
things that have happened in the past
Our town history is very interesting.

hit (hitting, hit)
to swing your hand or something you are holding against something else
Hit the ball as hard as you can.

▶ **hit**

hobby (hobbies)
something that you enjoy doing in your spare time
My hobbies are skateboarding and listening to music.

▲ **hobby**

hockey
a game played by hitting a ball using wooden sticks
Hockey is a very fast game.

hold (holding, held)
to have something in your hands or arms
Hold my coat, please.

hole
an opening or an empty space
There's a hole in the bag.

holiday
1 a special day
It is a very special holiday.
2 a time when you do not have to work or go to school
School holidays start soon.

hollow

empty inside
The log is hollow.

hologram

a picture made with a laser
There is a hologram on the sticker.

home

the place where you live
What time will you get home?

homework

school work you do at home
I do my homework when I get home from school.

honey

a sweet, sticky food made by bees
Put honey in your yoghurt.

hood

a piece of clothing that covers your head, usually attached to a coat or jacket
Put your hood up, it's raining.

▷ **hood**

hoof (hooves)

the foot of an animal, such as a deer, horse or goat
Horses have very thick hooves.

hook

a piece of metal or plastic for hanging up or catching things
Hang your jacket on the hook.

hoop

a large ring of metal, wood or plastic
It's fun to play with hoops.

▼ **hoops**

hop (hopping, hopped)

1 to jump on one foot, or make a small jump with two feet
Can you hop on one foot?

hope (hoping, hoped)

to wish for something
I hope you have a good time.

horn

1 one of the hard, pointed things on an animal's head
Goats and cows have horns.
2 something that you push to make a noise
The horn is very loud.

▼ **horn**

horrible

bad or unpleasant
What a horrible colour.

horse

a large animal with four legs, a mane and a tail
My brother can ride a horse.

▲ **horse**

hospital

the place where sick or injured people go to get better
Have you ever stayed in hospital?

hot
at a very high temperature
Mercury is the hottest planet
because it is closest to the Sun.

hot dog
a sausage in a long bun
Would you like a hot dog?

hotel
a place people pay to stay .
There's a hotel on the beach.

hour
sixty minutes
The film is an hour long.

house
a building that people live in
My friend lives in the house
across the street.

human (human being)
a person, not an animal
Humans are very intelligent.

hump
a large bump
The camel has a large hump on
its back.

hungry
feeling that you need food
I'm hungry. What's for dinner?

hunt (hunting, hunted)
1 to look for something or
someone
We hunted everywhere for the
other shoe.
2 to try to catch wild animals
The owl hunted for mice
at night.

hurricane
a very strong wind storm
Hurricanes can cause lots of
damage.

▲ **hurricane**

hurry (hurrying, hurried)
to do something quickly
Hurry and get your coat.

hurt (hurting, hurt)
1 to cause pain or harm
The dentist won't hurt you.
2 to feel pain
My knee hurts.

husband
the man who a woman is
married to
Dad is Mum's husband.

▲ **hunt**

• Puzzle time •

Can you match A with B?

A	B
dishwasher	bedroom
bed	bathroom
shower	kitchen

answers
dishwasher/kitchen
wardrobe/bedroom
shower/kitchen

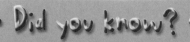

• Did you know? •
Owls have sharp claws called
talons which they use to grab
their prey.

huge
very big
There is a huge tent at the fair.

ice

water that is so cold that it has frozen and become hard
Do you want ice in your water?

▲ ice

iceberg

a large piece of ice that floats in the sea
Most of an iceberg is hidden under water.

▲ iceberg

· Did you know? ·

Very often just the 'tip of the iceberg' can be seen above the water's surface. Almost 90 percent is below the surface, making icebergs dangerous to ships.

ice cream

a frozen, sweet food that is usually made of milk or cream
Ice cream tastes good on hot days.

▲ ice cream

ice skate (ice skating, ice skated)

to move across ice wearing boots with a metal blade on the bottom
We're learning how to ice skate.

ice skating

icing

a sweet covering for cakes
Spread the icing evenly on the top of the cake.

▲ icing

idea

a plan or a thought about how to do something
Have you any ideas about how we can raise money for the school outing?

igloo

an Inuit house made of blocks of snow and ice
The Inuits only live in igloos in the winter.

▲ igloo

ill

not well, sick
I'm sorry to hear that you're ill.

imaginary

not real
The story is about an imaginary cat with special powers.

imitate (imitating, imitated)

to copy
He can imitate the way our teacher talks.

immediately

now, at once, right away
Please put your clothes away immediately.

important

1 serious, useful or valuable
It is a very important discovery.
2 powerful
The mayor is an important person in our town.

impossible
not able to be, be done or to happen
That's impossible – you can't be in two places at once!

information
facts or knowledge about someone or something
There is a lot of information about our school on our website.

initial
the first letter of a person's name
What is your middle initial?

injection
a way of putting medicine into your body using a special needle
The nurse comes to our school to give injections.

injure (injuring, injured)
to hurt or harm yourself or someone else
Luckily, no one was injured in the crash.

ink
coloured liquid that is used for writing, drawing or printing
Sign your name in ink.

◀ **ink**

insect
a small animal with six legs, wings and a body that has three parts
Beetles, butterflies and bees are all kinds of insects.

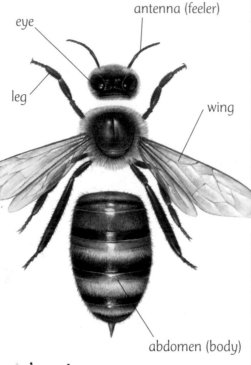

antenna (feeler)

eye

leg

wing

abdomen (body)

▲ **insect**

•Puzzle time•
There are three insect names hidden in this puzzle. Can you find them? Words are written vertically ↑ and horizontally →

t	r	b	e	e	o
s	d	l	e	f	w
e	u	a	y	a	a
c	a	n	d	d	s
a	e	t	r	o	p
z	x	c	t	n	o

answers
ant bee wasp

inside
in or into a place or container
Come inside the house, it's very cold out there.

instrument
something people use to do a job
We use instruments to make music.

triangle

tambourine

drum

guitar

▲ **instruments**

interested
wanting to pay attention to something or someone so that you can learn more
Sam is interested in sport.

interesting
exciting in a way that keeps your attention
Emailing children in other countries is really interesting.

Internet

a huge system of linked computers all over the world that lets people communicate with each other
We use the Internet at home and at school.

interrupt (interrupting, interrupted)

to break in or stop someone who is doing something or saying something
The phone call interrupted our conversation.

invade (invading, invaded)

to attack or go into a place in large numbers
The Vikings left their ships and invaded the country.

▼ **invade**

invent (inventing, invented)

to make something that has not been made before
Computers were invented about 65 years ago.

invention

something new that someone makes, or produces, for the first time
The telephone is the invention of Alexander Graham Bell.

car (1885)

telephone (1876)

light bulb (1879)

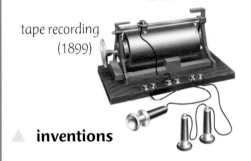

flying machine (1874)

tape recording (1899)

▲ **inventions**

invisible

not possible to see
You can't read it, it is written in invisible ink!

invite (inviting, invited)

to ask someone if they would like to do something such as come to a party
Ellie always invites lots of people to her parties.

invitation

a note or a card which asks you to go to a party
Have you replied to your party invitation?

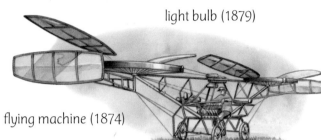

iron

1 a strong, hard metal
The machinery is made from iron.
▼ **iron**
2 a machine for smoothing clothes
Be careful, the iron gets very hot.

island

a piece of land that has water all around it
There are thousands of islands in the Pacific Ocean.

▲ **island**

Jj

jacket
a piece of clothing like a short coat
You should take a jacket with you.

▷ **jacket**

jail (or gaol)
a prison, a place where people are kept by the police
The thief was put in jail for seven months.

jam
a sweet food made from fruit
We sometimes have bread and jam for breakfast.

jar
a glass container for storing food
Jam and honey are sold in jars.

▲ **jar**

jealous
feeling angry or bad because you want something that someone else has
He is jealous of our grades.

jeans
trousers made of denim
My favourite clothes are jeans and a t-shirt.

▼ **jeans**

jelly
a clear, sweet solid food made from fruit juice
We have ice cream and jelly at birthday parties.

jellyfish
a sea animal that floats on the surface and can sting
There are many different types of jellyfish.

▷ **jellyfish**

jet
a fast aeroplane
There are several jet fighters in the air show.

▲ **jets**

jewellery
things such as necklaces, bracelets and earrings that you wear for decoration
She wore jewellery to the party.

▼ **jewellery**
earrings
bracelet
necklace

jigsaw
a puzzle made from shaped pieces that you fit together to make a picture
The jigsaw has 100 pieces.

▲ **jigsaw**

job
work that you get paid for doing
She has a new job.

join (joining, joined)
1 become a member of a club or other group
Lots of people join the Cubs and Brownies every year.
2 to stick or fasten together
Join the two pieces of card.

joke
a funny story that is told to make people laugh
Do you know any good jokes?

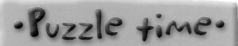
·Puzzle time·

Look at this joke. Use the code to find out what the answer is.

A B C D E F G H I J
1 2 3 4 5 6 7 8 9 10

K L M N O P Q R
11 12 13 14 15 16 17 18

S T U V W X Y Z
19 20 21 22 23 24 25 26

What did one road say to the other?
13/5/5/20 25/15/21 1/20
20/8/5   3/15/18/14/5/18!

Meet you at the corner!
answer

jolly
happy
He's a jolly person.

journey
a trip or the distance travelled
We were very tired after the long journey.

judo
a Japanese fighting sport
In judo, people try to throw each other to the floor.

jug
a container for liquids
Fill the jug with water.

▲ jug

juice
liquid from fruit or vegetables
You can have orange juice or apple juice.

▼ juice

jump (jumping, jumped)
to push yourself off the ground with both feet
Jump as high as you can.

▲ jump

jumper
a piece of clothing that covers your upper body that you pull over your head
That looks like a nice, warm jumper.

jungle
a thick forest in a hot country
The trees and plants in a jungle grow very close together.

▼ jungle

canopy

middle branches

forest floor

· Did you know? ·
There are more different kinds of animals and plants living in jungles than any other areas of the world.

just
to have happened a very short time ago
I've just got home from work.

Kk

kaleidoscope

a tube with pictures or pieces of coloured glass or plastic at one end that you look through and turn to see changing patterns
The kaleidoscope was invented in 1816.

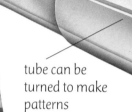

pattern

kangaroo

an Australian animal that keeps its young in a pocket on the front of its body
Kangaroos have big, strong back legs.

kangaroos

karate

a Japanese fighting sport
In karate, you fight using your hands and feet.

◀ **karate**

keep (keeping, kept)

1 to continue to have something
You can keep the library books for two weeks.
2 to continue to do something
Don't keep staring at that man.
3 to have something in a certain place
The paints and crayons are kept in the cupboard.

▼ **kaleidoscope**

tube can be turned to make patterns

coloured glass

kettle

a container or machine for boiling water
Come in, I'll put the kettle on and make some tea.

key

1 a special piece of metal used to open a lock
Turn the key to the right.
2 one of the parts of a computer or piano that you press with your fingers
Type the file name and then press the 'enter' key.
3 a set of answers or an explanation of symbols
There is a key at the back of the book.

◀ **key**

keyboard

the set of keys on a computer or a piano that you press to type or make a sound
This is a special keyboard with letters and pictures.

▲ **keyboard**

kick (kicking, kicked)

to swing your foot at something
Kick it into goal!

▲ **kick**

kill (killing, killed)

to cause someone or something to die
Some weeds kill other plants.

kind

helpful, pleasant and thoughtful
It's very kind of you to think of me.

king

a royal man who rules a country
Do you think the prince will become king?

▷ king

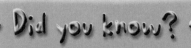
kiss (kissing, kissed)

to touch someone else with your lips
Mum kissed us all goodnight.

kitchen

the room in a house for preparing food
There are nice smells coming from the kitchen.

·Puzzle time·

How many kitchen things can you find in this word puzzle?

sinkovencupboardtable chairshelfcupandsaucer

8
answer

kite

a toy made of light wood and cloth, paper or plastic that you fly at the end of a long string
I like to fly my kite on windy days.

▲ kite

kitten

a baby cat
Our cat has two kittens.

▲ kittens

knee

the part of your leg that bends
When you walk on ice, you should bend your knees.

knife (knives)

a tool with a blade for cutting things into pieces
Put the knife to the right of your plate.

▲ knife

knit (knitting, knitted)

to join wool together with long metal sticks
Jodie can knit.

▽ knitting

knock (knocking, knocked)

to hit something to make a noise
Knock on the back door.

knot

the place where two pieces of string or rope are tied together
There are many different ways to tie knots.

▲ knot

Ll

label
a piece of paper or cloth which gives information about the thing it is attached to
Always put a label on your floppy disks.

lace
fine cloth made with patterns of tiny holes
The doll's dress is made of long, white lace.

▲ lace

ladder
a piece of equipment made from two long bars joined together by short bars, that is used for climbing up to reach high places
Dad uses a ladder when he paints the house.

ladybird
a round insect that is red with black spots
Ladybirds are good for the garden.

▲ ladybird

lake
a big area of water that has land all around it
The lake was surrounded by forests and mountains.

▲ lake

lamb
a young sheep or the meat from that animal
Lambs are born in the spring.

▲ lamb

lamp
a machine that gives light
Switch on the lamp, it's too dark to see.
◄ lamp

land
1 ground
We bought a plot of land.
2 the dry part of the Earth
The sailors were very happy to see land.
3 a place or a country
It is in a magical land far away.

land (landing, landed)
to reach the ground after being in the air
The plane lands at 2:45 p.m.

language
words used by people to communicate with each other
Our teacher speaks two languages, English and Chinese.

lap
1 the top of your legs when you are sitting down
My cat likes to sit on my lap when I'm reading.
2 once around a track
They ran 12 laps of the track.

large
big
We ate a large piece of cake.

laser
a powerful light or the machine that makes it
We saw a brilliant laser show at the museum.

last

1 after the others
We came last in the egg and spoon race.
2 the one that happened the shortest time ago
We went to Italy for our last holiday.

last (lasting, lasted)

to continue to work or to be
How long will the batteries last?

late

1 after the normal or correct time
Sorry I'm late!
2 towards the end of a period of time
It was late on Sunday afternoon.

laugh (laughing, laughed)

to make a sound that shows you are happy, or when you think something is funny
We laughed at Dad's silly joke.

▲ **laughing**

law

a rule made by the government
A new law has been passed.

lawn

a place in a garden or a park that is covered in grass that is cut short
Mow the lawn.

lay (laying, laid)

1 to put in a place
Lay the coats over the back of the chair.
2 to make an egg
The hens lay an egg most days.

lazy

1 a name given to someone who doesn't like work
She's the laziest girl in the class.
2 not busy, relaxed
We had a nice, lazy weekend.

lead (leading, led)

1 to show someone the way
The dog led them to the children.
2 to be in the front
The champion is leading the parade.

lean (leaning, leant, leaned)

1 to be in or move into a position that is not straight
Lean over the fence and pick up the ball.
2 to rest against something
Chris was leaning against the wall, watching the match.

leap (leaping, leapt)

to jump into the air or over something
The frog leapt into the pond.

▼ **leap**

learn (learning, learnt, learned)

to get knowledge or information about a subject
We are learning to paint pictures at school.

▲ **learn**

Ll

leave (leaving, left)
1 to go away from a place
What time are you leaving?
2 to put a thing in a place or to let a thing stay in a place
You can leave your bike in the garden.

leg
1 the part of your body that you stand up with, between your hip and your foot
Dad's legs are a lot longer than mine are.
2 the part of a table or chair that holds it up
One of the chair legs is broken.

lemon
a sour yellow fruit
We put lemon juice and sugar on the pancakes.

▲ lemon

lend (lending, lent)
to let someone have or use something which they will return after using
Lend me a pen, please.
also look at borrow

leopard
a large cat with yellow or white fur and black spots
Leopards are beautiful animals.

▲ leopard

leotard
a stretchy piece of clothing that you wear for dancing or exercising
We wear leotards in ballet class.

lesson
a time in which someone is taught something such as a skill or a subject
I go to extra French lessons every Thursday after school.

let (letting, let)
1 to allow someone to do something
Will your mum let you sleep over tonight?
2 to allow something to happen
Just let the ball fall.

letter
1 one of the signs of the alphabet used in writing
There are five letters in James's name.
2 a written message that you put in an envelope and send or give someone
You can either send a letter or an email.

•Puzzle time•

The words in this letter are backwards – what does the letter say?

raeD amdnarG,
I ma ta emoh yadot. I evah
a dloc. I epoh uoy era llew.
,evoL
kraM

answer
Dear Grandma, I am at home today. I have a cold. I hope you are well. Love, Mark

lettuce
a green, leafy vegetable eaten in salads
We're growing lettuce this year.

▲ lettuce

library
a place where books are kept
A mobile library comes to our village twice a week.

a b c d e f g h i j k l m

lick (licking, licked)
to put your tongue on something
Lick your ice cream, it's going to drip.

lie (lying, lay, lain)
to have your body flat on the floor, ground or bed.
We put our towels on the sand and lay down.

lie (lying, lied)
to say something that is not the truth
They lied about their age.

life (lives)
1 the time between when you are born and when you die
He had a long, happy life.
2 being alive
Do you think there is life on other planets?

lifeboat
a boat that helps people who are in danger at sea
The fishermen were rescued by the lifeboat just in time.

▼ **lifeboat**

lift
1 a machine that takes you up and down in a building
Take the lift to the fourth floor.
2 a ride in a car
Can we give you a lift?

lift (lifting, lifted)
to move something to a higher place
It took two people to lift our piano.

light
1 energy or brightness from the Sun or a lamp that lets you see things
Is there enough light to take a picture?
2 a machine that makes light
Turn off the light, it's time for bed.

◀ **light**

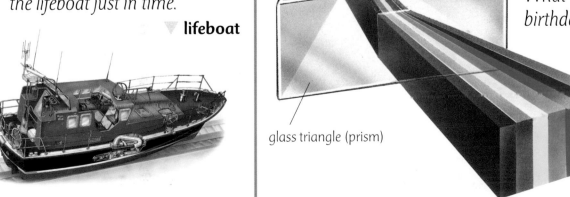

white light

glass triangle (prism)

light splits into the seven colours of the rainbow as it passes through the prism

lighthouse
a tower on the coast that has a bright light that flashes to warn ships
There's a lighthouse at the end of the beach.

lightning
electrical light in the sky during a storm.
We could see lightning in the distance.

▲ **lightning**

like (liking, liked)
1 to enjoy something or be fond of someone or something
I really like skateboarding.
2 to want
What would you like for your birthday?

line

1 a long, thin mark
Draw a line through the mistakes.
2 a piece of string, rope or wire
Hang the clothes on the line.
3 a row
There is a line of trees as you go into the park.

lion

a large wild cat
Lions live in Africa.

▼ **lion**

lips

the edges of your mouth
The cat came in, licking his lips.

liquid

something, such as water, that is not hard and can be poured
There's some liquid soap in the bathroom.

listen (listening, listened)

to pay attention to sound
Sorry, what did you say? I wasn't listening.

litter

1 rubbish lying on the ground
We picked up all the litter in the playground.
2 the group of babies that an animal has at one time
Our dog had a litter of puppies last night.

little

small, not large or not much
We gave the cat a little milk.

live (living, lived)

1 to be alive
My great grandfather lived to be 80 years old.
2 to have your home in a certain place
They live in France now.

•Puzzle time•

Can you fill in the missing letters to find out what is in the living room?

a. s _ _ a

b. t_l_v_si_n

c. b_ _ k she_f

d. a_mch_ir

e. la_p

answers
a. sofa b. television c. bookshelf
d. armchair e. lamp

living room

a room in a house for sitting and relaxing in
The TV is in the living room.

lizard

a short, four-legged animal that lays eggs
Lizards' blood changes temperature to match the temperature around it.

▲ **lizard**

loaf (loaves)

something such as bread that is baked in one piece
Get a loaf of bread and some milk from the shop.

lobster

a sea animal with eight legs, and two claws
We saw a lobster through the glass bottom of the boat.

▲ **lobster**

lock

an object that is used to close something, usually opened and shut with a key
There's a lock on the chest.

lock (locking, locked)
to close or fasten something with a key
Have you locked the door?

loft
the inside of the roof of a house
There's an old tennis racket in the loft.

log
a thick piece of a tree
It's cold in here, put another log on the fire.

▲ logs

lonely
feeling sad that you are on your own
Come over if you get lonely.

long
1 measuring a big distance from one end to the other
Is it a long walk?
2 continuing for a large amount of time
It's a very long movie.

look (looking, looked)
to pay attention to something that you see
Look at that hot air balloon.

loose
1 not tight
Wear loose clothes.
2 free to move
The lions were set loose.

lose (losing, lost)
1 to not be able to find something
He keeps losing his glasses.
2 to not win a competition or a game
Our team lost the competition.

loud
not quiet, making a lot of noise
Turn it down, that's too loud!

love (loving, loved)
to like someone or something very much
We love our new baby.

lovely
very beautiful or pleasant
It's a lovely day.

low
close to the ground, not high
There are some low clouds around the hills.

lucky
1 fortunate, having good things happen to you
They're lucky they won.
2 giving good luck
These are my lucky football boots.

lunch
a meal that you eat in the middle of the day
Why don't we meet for lunch?

▼ lunch

lungs
parts of your body inside your chest that help you to breathe
You have two lungs protected by bones called ribs.

▼ lungs

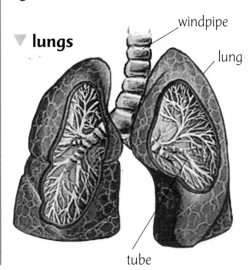

windpipe
lung
tube

Mm

machine

a piece of equipment that is used to do a job
Washing machines wash, rinse and spin your clothes.

▲ **machine**

magic

a power to make strange things happen
I can do magic tricks.

magnet

a piece of metal that makes some other metal objects move towards it
Use a magnet to pick up all the pins.

▲ **magnet**

main

the most important or the biggest
We'll meet you in front of the main entrance.

make (making, made)

1 to create or build something
The computer was made in a factory.
2 to cause something to happen or be a certain way
That joke always makes me laugh.

male

a man, boy or an animal that cannot produce eggs or have babies
Male elephants are bigger than female elephants.

mammal

the group of animals that give birth to live babies and make milk for them to drink
The blue whale is the largest mammal.

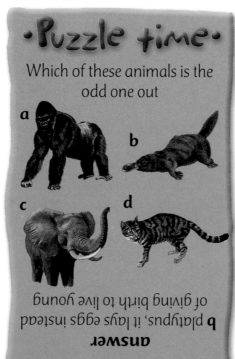

·Puzzle time·

Which of these animals is the odd one out

a
b
c
d

answer
b platypus, it lays eggs instead of giving birth to live young

man (men)

an adult male
That is a men's shop.

many

large in number
There are many good reasons to use the Internet.

map

a drawing that shows where things are in a building, town, country or other place
We studied a map of the world.

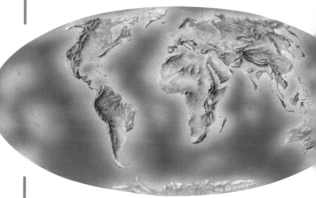
▲ **map**

marble

1 a type of hard stone
The walls are marble.
2 a small glass or metal ball used to play a game
I won two marbles in that last game.

▼ **marbles**

march (marching, marched)

to walk with regular steps
The band marched at the front of the parade.

mark

1 a sign or shape
Put a mark to show where your house is.
2 a letter or number that a teacher puts on a piece of work to show how good it is
She's getting really good marks this term.
3 a spot or a dark patch on something that makes it look bad
There is a mark on the carpet where we spilled the juice.

market

a place where you can buy food, clothes, plants and other things
Most markets are outdoors.

▲ **market**

marmalade

jam that is made from oranges
We had toast and marmalade for breakfast.

marry (marrying, married)

to become husband and wife
They married three years ago.

◀ **married**

mask

something that you put over your face to hide or protect it
He always wore a mask.

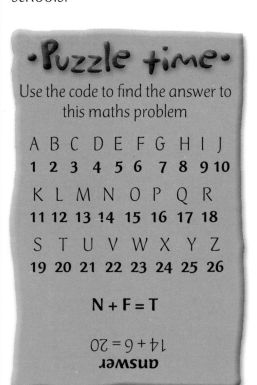

▶ **mask**

mat

a piece of material that covers a floor or table
Wipe your feet on the mat.

match (matches)

1 a small stick that makes a flame when you rub it against something
We have special long matches for lighting the fire.
2 a contest or game
That's the best football match I've ever seen.

▼ **matches**

mathematics (maths)

the study of numbers or shapes
Mathematics is studied in schools.

•Puzzle time•

Use the code to find the answer to this maths problem

A	B	C	D	E	F	G	H	I	J
1	2	3	4	5	6	7	8	9	10

K	L	M	N	O	P	Q	R
11	12	13	14	15	16	17	18

S	T	U	V	W	X	Y	Z
19	20	21	22	23	24	25	26

$$N + F = T$$

answer
$14 + 6 = 20$

meadow

a field with grass and flowers
The meadow was covered in pretty flowers.

▼ meadow

meal

a time when food is eaten or the food itself
Sometimes you feel sleepy after a big meal.

mean

1 cruel or unkind
Don't be mean to each other.
2 not wanting to spend money
He's very mean – maybe that's why he's rich.

meaning

the information that is supposed to be understood from words and signs
What is the meaning of this sentence?

measles

an illness that gives you a temperature and lots of red spots
My little brother has measles.

measure (measures, measuring, measured)

to find out the size or amount of something
Measure each side of the room.

meat

food made from animals
people who don't eat meat are called vegetarians.

mechanic

a person who fixes cars and machines
He's a good mechanic.

medal

a piece of metal which is given as a prize for winning a competition or for doing something special
He won a medal for bravery.

▶ medal

medicine

1 something that you take when you are not well so that you will get better
You have to take this medicine three times a day.
2 the study of illness and injury
She is studying medicine.

medium

a middle size between large and small
I'd like a medium popcorn, please.

meet (meeting, met)

1 to know someone for the first time
We met the first day of school.
2 to go to the same place as another person
Where shall we meet?

melody (melodies)

a song or the tune of a song
The song has a strange but beautiful melody.

melon

a fruit with a hard skin and flat seeds
Melons can be green, yellow or orange.

▶ melon

melt (melting, melted)
to change from a solid to a liquid when heated
The ice melted in the heat.

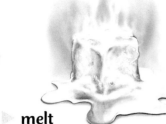

▶ **melt**

memory (memories)
1 something that you remember from the past
Photographs bring back memories.
2 the ability to remember things
Do you have a good memory?
3 the part of a computer where information is stored
This computer has more memory than our old one.
also look at remember and remind

mend (mending, mended)
to repair
Could you help me mend the tyre?

▲ **mend**

menu
1 the list of food in a café or restaurant
The waiter brought us each a menu.
2 a list of things seen on a computer screen
Click here to go back to the main menu.

messy
not tidy
This room is very messy.

message
information for a person from someone else
Leave a message for him on the note pad.

metal
hard material such as gold, silver, copper or iron
Silver is a precious metal.

▲ **metal**

microphone
something that is used for recording sounds or making them louder
Speak into the microphone.

▶ **microphone**

microscope
something that makes small things look much bigger
We looked at a hair under the microscope.

▶ **microscope**

microwave
an oven that cooks food very quickly using waves of electricity, not heat
Put the soup in the microwave for six minutes.

▲ **microwave**

midday
12:00 in the middle of the day
We'll have our lunch early – at about midday.

middle
the centre or the part of something that is between the beginning and the end
We sat down in the middle of the row.

midnight
12:00 in the middle of
the night
*We stay up until midnight on
New Year's Eve.*

mild
1 not too strong or serious
She had a mild case of flu.
2 not tasting too strong or
too spicy
It's a mild curry.
3 not too cold
The weather is mild today.

milk
white liquid
that female
humans and
other mammals
produce to feed
their babies
*We drink cow's
and goat's milk.*

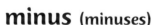
▷ **milk**

minus (minuses)
1 the sign used in maths
when taking one number
away from another
*Twenty-five minus five equals
twenty.*
2 in temperature, below zero
It's cold out there, minus 7!

$$25 - 5 = 20$$

▲ **minus**

minute
sixty seconds
*We waited for twenty minutes
but they didn't come.*

mirror
special glass that you can
see your reflection or
what's behind you in
*Go look in the mirror – you
look really funny.*

▷ **mirror**

miserable
very unhappy
*Don't look so
miserable.*

miss
not to hit a target
He missed the basket.

mistake
something that is wrong
We all make mistakes.

mittens
gloves that do not have
separate places for
each finger
*Wrap up well and
wear your mittens.*

◁ **mittens**

mix (mixing, mixed)
to put different things
together
Mix the eggs and flour together.

**mobile
phone**
a small
telephone that
people can carry
around
*Call me on the
mobile phone.*

▲ **mobile phone**

model
1 a small copy of something
such as a
plane or
a building
*We made a
model plane
at the
weekend.*
2 a person whose job
is to show clothes
She wants to be a model.
3 one type of something
*This computer is the most up
to date model.*

▷ **model**

money
coins and paper that you use to buy things with
Have you spent all your money already?

▲ money

monitor
the part of a computer that shows the screen
It's easier to see on a big monitor.

monkey
an animal with a long tail that uses its legs to climb
We watched the monkeys at the zoo.

▼ monkey

monster
a frightening creature in stories and films
The monster chased them into the forest.

◄ monster

month
one of the twelve parts of the year
Most months are 30 or 31 days long, except February.

Moon
the small planet that travels around the Earth
The Moon is full tonight.

▶ Moon

more (most)
1 stronger or greater than
This book is more interesting than the last one I read.
2 a larger or an additional amount or number
Is there any more cake?

morning
the part of the day between the time the sun comes up and noon
We get up at the same time every morning.

mosque
a building where Muslim people go to pray
The mosque is in the centre of the town.

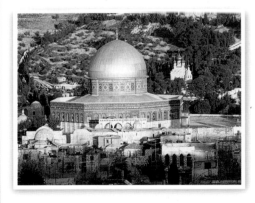

▲ mosque

moth
an insect that is similar to a butterfly
Moths are more active at night.

▶ moth

mother
a woman who has a child or a female animal that has young
My mother is a nurse.

motor
the part of a machine that uses power to make it work
There is a motor in the washing machine.

motorbike (motorcycle)
a vehicle with two wheels and a seat for people to ride on
Dad has a new motorbike.

▲ **motorbike**

mountain
land that has been pushed up very high
Some mountains have snow on top all year round.

▲ **mountain**

mouse (mice)
1 a small animal with a long tail and a pointed nose
There are mice in the field.
2 the part of a computer with a ball in it that you move by hand to move things around on the screen
You can play this game using a mouse.

▲ **mouse**

·Puzzle time·

Can you spot five differences between these two pictures?

answers
1 flag 2 scarf 3 moustache 4 smoke 5 moon

moustache
the hair that grows above a man's lip
He has a little moustache.

mouth
the part of your face that you use to talk and eat
Don't talk with your mouth full.

move (moving, moved)
to change the position of something
Could you move, please, I can't see the TV.

movie
a story that is told using pictures that move, a film
What movie would you like to see tonight?

much
a lot
Thank you very much for inviting me.

mud
wet soil or earth
The rugby players were covered in mud.

▲ **mud**

mug

a cup with tall sides
Do you want a mug of hot chocolate?

▲ **mug**

multiply (multiplies, multiplying)

to add a number to itself, often more than once
four multiplied by two is eight.

▼ **multiply**

$$4 \times 2 = 8$$
$$3 \times 3 = 9$$
$$3 \times 4 = 12$$
$$7 \times 2 = 14$$

mumps

an illness that makes your neck swell
Have you had mumps?

munch (munches, munching, munched)

to eat something noisily
The rabbit munched on carrots and lettuce.

muscle

one of the parts of the body that tightens and relaxes to cause movement
Relax your muscles.

▼ **muscles**

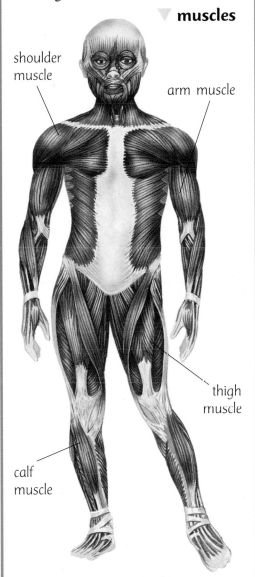

shoulder muscle

arm muscle

thigh muscle

calf muscle

• **Did you know?** •
The human body has about 620 muscles that are used thousands of times every day. For instance, you use about 200 muscles every time you take a single step, and the tiny muscles that move your eyes are used up to 100,000 times a day!

museum

a place where old, important, valuable or interesting things are kept so that people can go and look at them
There is a toy museum, a science museum and an art museum.

mushroom

a small vegetable that has a stem with a round top
Do you want mushrooms on your pizza?

▼ **mushrooms**

music

a pattern of sounds that is sung or played on special instruments
Can you read music?

▲ **music**

must

to have to do something
You must lock the door before going to bed at night.

mysterious

something strange, secret or difficult to understand
He is a mysterious person, we don't know much about him.

Nn

nail
1 a thin, sharp piece of metal with one flat end that you hit with a hammer
Hang the picture on that nail.
2 the hard covering on the ends of your fingers and toes
He bites his nails.

▲ nails

name
what a person or object is called
What's your name?

narrow
having only a short distance from one side to the other
The road is very narrow.

▲ narrow

nasty
very unpleasant or bad
That's a nasty cut.

nation
a country and the people who live there
It is a poor nation.

naughty
badly behaved
My little sister can be very naughty.

·Puzzle time·

Someone has been naughty, and written this message backwards. Can you work out what it says?

ouy dlouhs od ruoy krowemoh yreve yad.

answer
you should do your homework every day.

navy
the ships and people that fight for a country at sea during a war
My cousin is in the navy.

near
close by, not far
There's a bus stop near the zoo.

neat
1 clean or organised
His room is always neat and tidy.
2 clearly presented
You have very neat handwriting.

neck
the part of your body that attaches your head to your shoulders
Put a scarf around your neck.

necklace
a piece of jewellery that you wear around your neck
That's a beautiful necklace.

▲ necklace

needle
1 a thin, sharp piece of metal, with a hole through it used for sewing
First, thread the needle.
2 a thin, sharp piece of metal through which injections are given
The needle will not hurt you.

▲ needle

neighbour

a person who lives near another person
We invited all our friends and neighbours to the party.

nephew

the son of your sister or brother
My nephew is staying with us for a few days.

also look at family

nervous

worried or frightened, not able to relax
She's a little nervous about being in the school play.

nest

a place birds make to lay their eggs
There's a robin's nest in that tree.

▼ **nest**

• Did you know? •
The weaver bird's nest is a work of art. Using its beak, it weaves straw and grass into a large nest with its own roof and entrance!

net

material that is made by joining pieces of string or thread together, leaving spaces between them
We use a small net when we go fishing.

▲ **net**

network

a system of things or people that are connected.
There's a computer network at school .

never

not at any time, not ever
I've never been to China.

new

not old or used
Is that a new jacket?

news

information about something that is happening now or that happened a short time ago
Write soon and send us all your news.

newspaper

sheets of paper that are printed with words and pictures to tell you what is happening in the world.
Have you read today's newspaper?

▲ **newspapers**

next

the one that is nearest or immediately after another one
Who's next on the list?

nice

enjoyable, good, pleasant
Did you have a nice time?

niece

the daughter of your sister or brother
Her niece works in a bank.

night

the time of day between when the sun sets and rises again
The moon can be seen at night.

▼ **night**

nightgown (nightie)

a dress to sleep in
Put your nightgown on and get into bed.

nightmare

a bad dream
Nightmares can be very scary.

nobody

no one, no person
There's nobody home.

nod (nodding, nodded)

to quickly move your head up and down
She nodded her head in reply.

noise

loud sounds
Keep the noise down, will you?

none

not any, not one
Sorry, there is none left in the box.

nonsense

something that does not make any sense, or mean anything
The television programme was complete nonsense.

noodles

very thin strips of food that are usually made from flour, water and eggs then boiled
Do you want rice or noodles?

▲ **noodles**

noon

midday, 12:00
Let's meet at noon.

no one

nobody, not one person
I have no one to talk to.

nose

the part of your face that you use for breathing and smelling things
Breathe in deeply through your nose.

• Did you know? •

When we smell something, scent particles go into our nose, which sends messages to our brain. If something makes us sneeze, the rush of air out of the nose can reach 160 kilometres per hour!

▼ **nose**

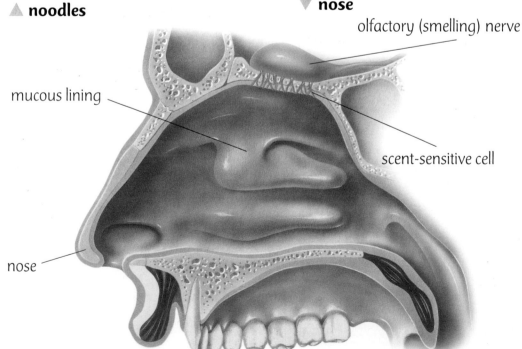

olfactory (smelling) nerve

mucous lining

scent-sensitive cell

nose

note

1 a short written message
Mother wrote a note to the school.
2 a piece of paper money
We paid with notes and coins.
3 a musical sound or the mark to show a musical sound
The opera singer can hit very high notes.

▲ **note**

nothing

not any thing, zero
There's nothing in the box, it's empty.

notice (noticing, noticed)

1 to see something, or be aware that it is there
Did you notice anyone there?
2 a sign that tells people something
The notice says the play starts tonight.

now

this time, the present
Where are you going now?

number

1 a word or symbol that means the amount, quantity or order of something
Some people think seven is a lucky number.
2 the numbers you press on a phone to call someone
Have you got our new number?

```
 1 = one
 2 = two
 3 = three
 4 = four
 5 = five
 6 = six
 7 = seven
 8 = eight
 9 = nine
10 = ten
```

nurse

a person whose job is to take care of people who are sick or hurt
Go and see the school nurse, you don't look well.

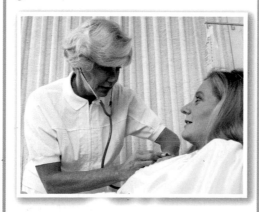

▲ **nurse**

nursery (nurseries)

1 a place where small children are looked after during the day
My little brother still goes to nursery.
2 a place where plants are grown and sold
We bought some beautiful plants at the nursery on the hill.

nursery rhyme

a poem or song for young children
My favourite nursery rhyme is 'Jack and Jill'.

•Puzzle time•

What are the missing words?

a. Jack and Jill went up the – – – –

b. Humpty – – – – – – sat on a wall

c. Mary, Mary, quite – – – – – – – –

d. Little Miss _ _ _ _ _ _ sat on a tuffet

answers
a. hill b. Dumpty c. contrary d. Muffet

nut

a seed that you can eat
Peanuts, cashews and almonds are all different types of nuts.

ocean

1 the salt water that covers most of the Earth
Strange fish live at the bottom of the ocean.
2 a large sea
The Pacific Ocean is the largest ocean.

• Did you know? •

About 97 percent of all the water on Earth is in the oceans. The Pacific is the biggest ocean. It is twice as big as the next largest ocean, the Atlantic. This is followed by the Indian, Southern and Arctic Oceans.

octopus

a sea animal that has eight legs
The legs of the octopus are called tentacles.

▶ **octopus**

off

1 not on
Take the glass off the table.
2 not in use or switched on
Shut the computer down before you switch it off.
3 away from
Keep off the grass.

office

a place where people work at desks
There are 34 people in my Mum's office.

oil

1 a thick liquid made from plants or animals and used for cooking
Put a little olive oil in the pan.
2 a thick liquid that comes out of the ground and is used to make petrol
They discovered oil there last year.
3 a thick liquid that is used on metal or wood so that parts move better or more easily
This door is squeaking. Can you put some oil on it, please?

OK (okay)

1 fine, healthy, well
Are you okay?
2 all right
Is it okay if I copy my work to your computer?

old

not young, not new
My grandad is getting very old.

▲ **old**

once

1 one time
We've met only once.
2 one time in a fixed period
We go swimming once a week.

onion

a vegetable that has a strong smell and taste
Do you want onion on your pizza?

▶ **onions**

open

not closed or covered over
What time does the shop open?

operation

when a doctor cuts open a person's body to mend or remove something
The operation took two hours.

opposite

1 completely different
The opposite of near is far.
2 across from, facing
They live in the house opposite.

orange

a fruit that grows on trees and is the colour between red and yellow

Would you like some orange juice?

orange

orbit (orbiting, orbited)

to travel round and round something, like a planet in space
The Earth orbits the Sun.

orchestra

a group of people playing musical instruments together
He plays violin with the school orchestra.

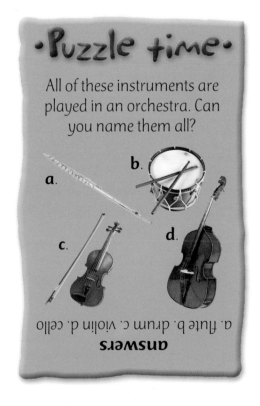

•Puzzle time•

All of these instruments are played in an orchestra. Can you name them all?

a.
b.
c.
d.

a. flute b. drum c. violin d. cello
answers

order

1 to ask for something in a restaurant, shop or on the Internet
Can I order a coffee, please?
2 to tell someone what to do
The captain ordered the men to attack the ship.

ordinary

not special, normal
It's just an ordinary house.

ostrich

a large, African bird with a long neck
Ostriches cannot fly.

otter

a brown, furry wild animal that swims and eats fish
Otters are rarely seen.　　otter

out

1 not in
The mouse got out of his cage.
2 not at home
She's out at the moment.
3 out of — none left
We're out of sugar.

outdoors

not inside a building, in the open air
It's much cooler outdoors.

oven

something that you use to bake or roast food
Bake the cake in the oven.

▲ **oven**

over

1 above, covering
He put a blanket over us.
2 finished, ended
Is the film over yet?
3 from one side to another
A bridge runs over the river.

owl

a bird that hunts at night
Sometimes you can hear an owl hooting.

also see hunt

own (owning, owned)

to have something that you bought or were given
We own a new house.

oxygen

a gas that animals and plants need to live
There is an oxygen mask above your seat.

Pp

pack (packing, packed)
to put things into boxes, bags or suitcases
Don't forget to pack your suitcases.

▲ **pack**

package
a small parcel
This package has your name on it.

•Puzzle time•

How many words can you make using the letters from this word?

packages

You should be able to make at least six!

paddle (paddling, paddled)
1 to move a boat through water using oars or your hands
They paddled the canoe across the lake.
2 to walk in shallow water
My little brother can't swim yet, but he likes to paddle.

▼ **paddle**

page
one side of a sheet of paper in a book, magazine or newspaper
This book has 128 pages.

pain
the feeling you have when you are hurt or ill
I have a bad pain in my side.

paint
a sticky liquid that you brush onto things to colour them
Don't spill paint on the carpet.

pair
1 two things that go together
I need a new pair of trainers.
2 something that is made of two similar things joined together
I've bought a new pair of sunglasses for my holiday.

▲ **pair**

•Puzzle time•

Which things do we talk about in pairs? Can you find all the pairs in this picture?

answers
jeans socks gloves
scissors trainers

◄ **paint**

palace
a large, especially fine house where a king, queen or other important person lives
The palace is surrounded by beautiful gardens.

▲ palace

palm
1 the inside part of your hand
Fortune-tellers read palms.
2 a kind of tree with leaves only at the top
Our tent was under a row of palms on the beach.
also look at hand

pan
a round cooking pot that usually has a long handle
Melt the butter in a large pan.

◄ pan

pancake
a thin, flat cake that is cooked in a frying pan
I like pancakes with sugar.

panda
a large, black and white animal that looks like a bear
Pandas come from China.

◄ panda

pantomime
a funny musical show for children that is performed around Christmas time
The pantomime this year is 'Robin Hood'.

paper
1 thin sheets of material for writing or printing on
There is no paper in the printer.
2 a newspaper
We recycle our newspapers once a week.

parachute
a piece of equipment made of cloth that people wear to let them fall slowly through the air
The parachute will open automatically.

► parachute

parade
a number of people walking or marching in a long line to celebrate a special occasion
There is a parade every year.

▲ parade

parent
a mother or father
We're making a special dinner for our parents.

park
a piece of ground with trees and grass, usually in a town
Let's go to the park to play.

park (parking, parked)
to put a car, truck, bus or bike in a place for a time
You can park right in front of the library.

parrot

a tropical bird with coloured feathers
Nadia's parrot can say her name.

▶ **parrot**

part

1 one of the pieces or sections that something is divided into
Would you like part of my orange?
2 the role of an actor in a film or a play
Who is playing the part of the princess?

party (parties)

a group of people gathered together to enjoy themselves
The party is on Saturday.

▼ **party**

pass (passing, passed)

1 to go beyond or past a person, place or thing
You'll pass the bakery on your way.
2 to succeed in doing something such as a test or an examination
I hope you pass your driving test.
3 to give someone something
Please pass the strawberries.

passenger

someone who travels in a vehicle that is controlled by someone else
This aeroplane has seats for 48 passengers.

Passover

a Jewish holiday held in the spring.
All of the family get together for Passover.

also look at holiday

past

1 after
Let's meet at half past six.
2 up to and beyond
The bank is on this street, just past the supermarket.
3 the time before the present
In the past, there was no such thing as email.

pasta

food made from flour, eggs and water, cut into shapes
Pasta is easy to cook.

▲ **pasta**

paste

1 a type of glue that is used for sticking paper
You can make paste with flour and water.
2 a soft, spreadable mixture
He likes fish paste sandwiches.

patch (patches)

1 a piece of material to cover a hole in something
I put a patch on my jeans.
2 a small piece of land
We have a vegetable patch this summer.

•Puzzle time•

What grows in a vegetable patch? Unscramble the names of these vegetables to find out

a. tscrrao **b.** bbcaaseg
c. ttoomaes **d.** snaeb
e. shanicp

answers
a. carrots b. cabbages
c. tomatoes d. beans e. spinach

pattern

1 lines, shapes or colours arranged in a certain way
The pattern on the cushions matches the curtains.
2 a shape that you copy or use as a guide to make something
Mum used a pattern to make this jacket for me.

▲ **pattern**

pavement

the path you walk on next to a road
The cycle path runs between the pavement and the road.

paw

the foot of an animal
Our dog has a sore paw.

pay (paying, paid)

to give someone money for something you are buying, or because someone has done work
I'll pay for their tickets.

pea

a small, round green seed that is eaten as food
Would you like peas with your dinner?

▲ **peas**

peace

1 no war or fighting
There has been peace between them for many years.
2 quiet, calmness
She shut the door for a little peace and quiet.

peach (peaches)

a soft fruit with a large seed inside it
This is a sweet, juicy peach.

▲ **peaches**

peacock

a male bird with long, brightly coloured tail feathers that spread out like a fan
Peacocks usually have green and blue feathers.

peanut

a small nut with a soft, bumpy shell
Those peanuts taste very salty.

▲ **peanuts**

pedal

1 part of a bicycle that you push with your feet to make the wheels go round
Can you reach the pedals?
2 part of a car that you push with your feet to make it stop and go
The brake pedal is for stopping the car.

peel (peeling, peeled)

to take the skin off a fruit or a vegetable
I helped peel the potatoes.

pen

an object for drawing and writing with ink
Sign this with a black pen.

▲ **pen**

pencil

an object used for drawing and writing that has lead, not ink, in it
Do the crossword with a pencil.

◀ **pencils**

penguin

a black and white sea bird than cannot fly
Penguins use their wings to help them swim.

▼ **penguins**

· Did you know? ·

Penguins usually have one or two eggs at a time. Both parents take turns in keeping the eggs warm. Later, the young penguins are looked after in groups, usually by the male bird.

penny (pence)

one pence
These sweets are a penny each.

pepper

1 a hot powder used to flavour food
Please pass the salt and pepper.
2 a sweet or hot-tasting vegetable
Peppers may be green, red, yellow or orange.

▼ **peppers**

perfume

a liquid with a pleasant smell that you put on your skin
What perfume are you wearing?

person (people, persons)

a human being, a man, woman or child
Our geography teacher is a very interesting person.

pet

an animal that is kept at someone's home
Do you have any pets?

petrol

liquid fuel that makes a car engine run
We need to stop for petrol.

phone

a telephone
Could you answer the phone, please?

phone (phoning, phoned)

to call someone on the telephone
Joe phoned while you were out.

photo (photograph)

a picture made with a camera
We had our photos taken for our passports.

piano

a musical instrument with black and white keys that you press to make sounds
A piano has 88 keys.

▶ **piano**

pick (picking, picked)

1 to choose
He was picked for the team.
2 to break off a flower or a piece of fruit from a plant
We picked a kilo of strawberries.
3 to pull pieces off or out of something
Pick the chicken off the bones.

picnic

food that you take outdoors to eat
We had a picnic in the park.

▼ **picnic**

picture
a drawing, painting or photograph
The winner's picture will be in the paper.

pie
food made with fruit, vegetables, fish or meat that is baked inside pastry
Would you like another piece of pie?

▲ pie

piece
a part of something that has been separated or broken
Careful, there are some pieces of glass on the floor.

pig
a farm animal with pink skin, short legs, a fat body and a curly tail
A baby pig is called a piglet.

▲ pigs

pile
a lot of things put on top of each other
There's a pile of clothes on the floor.

pillow
a cushion to put your head on in bed
I put my tooth underneath my pillow.

pilot
the person who is in control of a plane
The pilot showed us the plane's control panel.

pin
a sharp, thin piece of metal that is used to fasten things or hold pieces of cloth together
Take all the pins out before you try that on.

pineapple

a brown fruit that is yellow inside and has pointed leaves that stick out of the top
Pineapple juice is sweet.

▲ pineapple

pirate
a person who goes onto boats and ships to steal the things they are carrying
The ship was attacked by a group of pirates.

•Puzzle time•
Where has the pirate buried the treasure? Use the code to find out:

A	B	C	D	E	F	G	H	I	J
1	2	3	4	5	6	7	8	9	10

K	L	M	N	O	P	Q	R
11	12	13	14	15	16	17	18

S	T	U	V	W	X	Y	Z
19	20	21	22	23	24	25	26

21 /14/4/5/18
20/8/5   16/1/12/13
20/18/5/5

answer
under the palm tree

pizza
a thin, flat round bread that is covered with tomatoes, cheese and other toppings then baked in an oven
We're going to have pizza at the party.

▲ pizza

place
where something is, the position, point or other location
There is a special place, deep in the forest.

plain
1 one colour, having no pattern or decoration
The curtains are plain green.
2 easy to understand
Can you tell me in plain English?
3 not fancy or complicated
It's a plain room, but very clean and neat.

plan
1 an idea about what will happen in the future
We have holiday plans.
2 a drawing of a room, building or other space
We drew a plan for our perfect playground.

plan (planning, planned)
to think about what you want to do and how to do it
We're planning a party.

plane
an aeroplane
The plane took off from the airport on time.

planet
one of the very large, round objects that moves around the Sun
There are nine planets in our Solar System.

Pluto

Neptune

Uranus

Saturn

Jupiter

Earth

Mars

Mercury

Venus

▲ planets

plant
a living thing that has roots, leaves and seeds and can make its own food
Water the plant every day.

plant (planting, planted)
to put seeds or plants into the ground or containers so they will grow
Plant the seeds in early summer.

plaster
1 a very thick paste which hardens when it dries
Plaster is used to cover walls inside buildings.
2 a thin piece of plastic or cloth that you put over a cut or sore
I have a plaster on my knee.

plastic
a light material that is made from chemicals
The bucket is made of plastic.

plate
a flat dish to eat food from
Take the plates into the kitchen.

▲ plates

play
a story performed by actors in a theatre or on the radio
'The Tempest' is a play full of magical things.

play (playing, played)
to do things that you like such as games or sports
Let's play outdoors.

▲ play

playground
a place for children to play
There are swings and a slide at the playground.

please
a word to use when you are asking for something politely
Please wait here.

plenty
enough or more than enough
Have one of my sandwiches, I have plenty.

plough
a piece of equipment that farmers use to turn the soil before they plant
Modern ploughs can cut through the earth very quickly.

▲ plough

plug
1 a piece of plastic or rubber that stops water going out of a sink or bath
Put the plug in the bath, then turn on the water.
2 a piece of plastic connected to an electrical wire that you put into a wall
Which one is the plug for the computer?

plumber
a person whose job is to fix water taps and pipes
The plumber repaired the leak.

plus (pluses)
and, added to, the symbol +
Eleven plus six equals seventeen.

$$11 + 6 = 17$$ plus

pocket
a small, flat bag sewn into a piece of clothing or luggage
Put your key in your pocket.

poem
writing that uses words which sound good together. The words may rhyme
This poem is very funny.

•Puzzle time•
Here is a scrambled poem. Can you put each line in the correct order?
Hint – each line begins with a word that has a capital letter.

a. Roses red are
b. are blue Violets
c. sweet is Sugar
d. And are you so

d. And so are you
c. Sugar is sweet
b. Violets are blue
a. Roses are red
answers

point

1 a sharp end on something
Use a pencil with a sharp point.
2 a certain place or time
There's a meeting point at the airport.
3 the reason for something
The whole point was to raise money for the school.
4 a mark for counting a score in a game
The answer is worth one point.

point (pointing, pointed)

to use your hand or finger to show someone something
Point to where the gate is

pole

1 a long narrow piece of wood, plastic or metal
We forgot to take the tent poles.

police

people whose job is to make everyone obey the law
Police officers work very hard.

polite

speaking or acting in a pleasant and not rude way
It is polite to say please, thank you and excuse me.

pond

a small area of water
There are fish in the pond.

pony (ponies)

a small horse
Dusty is a beautiful little pony.

▲ **pony**

pool

1 a place filled with water for swimming
I like playing in my pool when the weather is warm.
2 a puddle or another small area of water
We saw tiny, coloured fish in the pools on the beach.

▲ **pool**

poor

1 not having enough money
It's a very poor country.
2 not as good as it should be
The food was poor.

pop

1 a sudden noise
There was a loud pop when they opened the bottle.
2 a short form of popular
They are a famous pop band.
3 a fizzy drink
Do you want a bottle of pop?

porcupine

a wild animal with long needles on its back
Porcupine needles are called quills.

▲ **porcupine**

pork

meat from a pig
We're having pork chops for dinner tonight.

porridge

a warm breakfast food that is made from oats
I like honey on porridge.

post office

a place where people buy stamps and send letters.
Can you get me some stamps at the post office?

potato (potatoes)

a roundish white vegetable that grows under the ground
Potatoes have brown, yellow or red skins.

◀ potatoes

pour (pouring, poured)

to make a liquid move out of or into something
Pour the juce while I make breakfast.

▶ pour

powerful

1 having strength
A crocodile has powerful jaws.
2 able to control
It is one of the most powerful countries in the world.

practice

Something that you do again and again to improve a skill
What time is swimming practice tonight?

practise (practising, practised)

doing something regularly to improve a skill
Keep practising your serve.

pram

a little bed on wheels for moving a baby around
We're taking the baby out in the pram.

prepare (preparing, prepared)

to get ready or to make something ready
I'm preparing for the test.

present

present ▼

1 a gift, a thing that you are given without asking for it
Thank you for all the presents.
2 now
The story is set in the present.

president

the leader of an organisation or a country
She is president of the club.

press (pressing, pressed)

to push something
Press the space bar.

pretend (pretending, pretended)

to act like something is true when it is not
She pretended to be asleep.

pretty

pleasant to look at
What pretty flowers!

price

the amount of money that a thing costs
The prices are high.

prince

the son or grandson of a king or queen
Prince Charming found the glass slipper.

princess (princesses)

a daughter or the granddaughter of a king or queen
The princess dreamed of a faraway place.

▲ princess

print (printing, printed)
1 to put letters, numbers or pictures on paper with a machine
Print five copies of the story.
2 to write words without joining the letters together
Print your name in full.

printer
1 a machine connected to a computer that makes copies on paper
The printer is out of paper.
2 a person who runs a printing machine
Take the poster to the printer.

prison
a place where people are kept under guard as punishment
The thief was sent to prison.

prize
something that you win in a game or competition
The first prize is a holiday.

problem
1 something that is wrong and needs to be corrected
We have a problem with this floppy disk.
2 a question that needs to be answered
There are 25 problems in the maths test.

promise (promising, promised)
to tell someone that you will definitely do something
The boy promised he would be good.

protect (protecting, protected)
to take care of someone or something and not let it be hurt or damaged
The penguin protects its chick from danger.

protect

proud
feeling pleased or happy that you or someone else has done something, or has something
Her parents were very proud of her.

puddle
a little pool of water on the ground or floor
There were puddles on the pavement after the rain.

pull (pulling, pulled)
to move something towards you, in a certain direction or drag something behind you
We pulled on the rope as hard as we could.

pull

pump
a machine that moves a liquid or gas in a certain direction
Take your tyre pump with you.

puncture
a hole made by a sharp object, especially in a tyre
We had a puncture on the way home.

punish (punishing, punished)
to do something bad or unpleasant to someone because they have done something wrong
Don't punish him, it was an accident.

pupil

1 a school student
The pupils at school wear uniforms.
2 the black centre of your eye
Your pupil gets smaller when you look at bright light.
also look at eye

puppet

a toy that people move by putting their hand inside it or by pulling strings attached to it
There's a puppet show starting in 10 minutes.

▲ **puppet**

puppy (puppies)

a young dog
Puppies open their eyes when they are about two weeks old.

▲ **puppies**

pure

not mixed with anything else
This is pure apple juice.

purr

the soft, low sound a cat makes when it is happy
Our cat purrs when you scratch his ears.

purse

a bag to keep money in
I'll have to pay you later, I left my purse at home.

push (pushing, pushed)

1 to move something away from you or out of your way
He pushed past everyone.
2 to press down on something such as a key or a button
Push the restart button.

put (putting, put)

to move a thing to a place
Just put the bags over there.

pyjamas

loose clothes that you wear to bed
Have a warm bath and put on your pyjamas.

pyramid

1 a very old stone building with triangular walls that form a point at the top
The Egyptian pyramids were built 4,000 years ago.
2 something with this shape
The tent is pyramid-shaped.

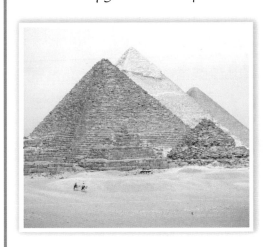

▲ **pyramids**

· **Did you know?** ·
It took 20,000 men more than 20 years to build the great Egyptian pyramids!

python

a large snake that kills animals for food by squeezing them
Some pythons grow to be eight metres long.

python

Qq

quarter
one of four equal, or nearly equal, parts of something
Divide the apple into quarters.

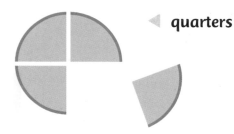
◀ **quarters**

queen
the royal female ruler of a country or the wife of a king
The Queen lives in a palace.

◀ **queen**

• Did you know? •
Elizabeth I (the first) was queen of England from 1558 to 1603. Her rule over England is often called 'the Golden Age' as it was a time of great achievement. During Elizabeth's reign, William Shakespeare wrote some of his finest poetry.

question
something that you ask someone
We'll try to answer all your questions.

queue
a line of people waiting
There was a long queue at the cinema.

quick (quickly)
fast
Email is quick and easy.

quiet (quietly)
1 not making noise
Please be quiet.
2 calm and still, not busy
The lake is quiet and peaceful this time of day .

quilt
a warm cover for a bed
Patchwork quilts are made by sewing lots of small pieces of cloth together.

▲ **quilt**

quit (quitting, quit)
to stop doing something or to leave a computer programme
To quit, press Ctrl + Q.

quiz
a game or competition that tests your knowledge
We have a quiz night every year at Scouts.

• Puzzle time •
Can you answer all the questions in this quiz?
Hint – the answers are all in this dictionary.
a. What is a baby pig called?
b. Can penguins fly?
c. Is a tomato a fruit or a vegetable?
d. What are the needles on a porcupine called?
e. How many hours are there in a day?

answers
a. piglet b. no c. a fruit d. quills e. 24

quote (quoting, quoted)
to repeat the words that someone else has said or written
The English teacher quoted a line from Shakespeare's 'Hamlet' to the class.

a b c d e f g h i j k l m

Rr

rabbit
a small furry animal with long ears
There are rabbits living in the wood.

▲ **rabbits**

race
1 a competition to see who can do something the fastest
The race starts in 15 minutes.
2 a group of people with the similar physical features
The goal is that people of all races and all beliefs can live together happily.

race (racing, raced)
1 to compete in a race
They're racing against some of the fastest runners in the world.
2 to do something very quickly
Jessie raced through the first part of the test.

racket (racquet)
1 a flat, hard net on the end of a stick that you use to play sports such as tennis, badminton and squash
These new tennis rackets are very light.
2 noise
Who's making all that racket?

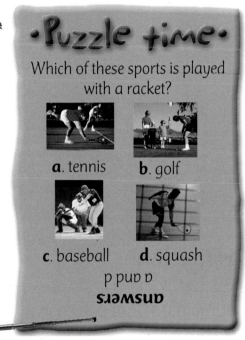
▲ **racket**

• **Puzzle time** •
Which of these sports is played with a racket?

a. tennis   **b.** golf

c. baseball   **d.** squash

answers
a and d

radio
a piece of equipment that receives sounds from the air
Before the Internet, people used to communicate by phone.
▲ **radio**

rail
1 a bar to hang things on or stop things from falling
Put your wet towel on the rail to dry.
2 one of two metal tracks that a train runs on
They put new rails all along the track.

railway
1 a train track
The railway runs to the coast.
2 a system of trains
A light railway is being built in the city.

rain
water that falls from clouds in the sky
It's been raining all day.

rainbow
the curve of colours that you see in the sky after it rains and the Sun comes out
The colours of the rainbow are red, orange, yellow, green, blue, indigo and violet.

▶ **rainbow**

raise (raising, raised)
to lift or put something in a higher place
Raise your hand if you know the answer.

rat
an animal that looks like a big mouse with a long tail
There are rats in the barn

▲ rat

rattle
a toy that makes a knocking noise when you shake it
Babies like rattles because they make a noise.

raw
not cooked
You can cook cabbage or eat it raw.

read (reading, read)
to understand words or symbols printed on a page
I like reading in the garden.

▲ read

record (recording, recorded)
to write down, tape or otherwise store information
We recorded our voices on the computer.

recycle (recycling, recycled)
to use something over again
We're recycling newspapers and magazines at school.

▲ recycle

reflection
an image, like a copy of something, that is seen in a mirror or water
We could see the reflection of the mountain in the water.

▼ reflection

refrigerator (fridge)
a machine to keep food cool
Put the milk back in the refrigerator.

▲ refrigerator

remember (remembering, remembered)
1 to keep information about the past in your mind
I remember how much fun we had then.
2 to bring back information to your mind
Oh! I just remembered – we're supposed to phone Gina!

remind (reminding, reminded)
to cause someone to remember something
Remind me to buy sugar.

repeat (repeating, repeated)
to say or do something again
Sorry, could you repeat that – I didn't hear you.

rescue (rescuing, rescued)
to save someone or something from danger
The lifeguard rescued the children.

rest (resting, rested)
to not be active, to relax
I wasn't asleep, just resting.

restaurant
a place where people eat and pay for meals
There's a new Thai restaurant in town.

▲ restaurant

result
1 something that happens because of something else
This beautiful garden is the result of a lot of hard work.
2 a final score
Have you heard the latest football results?

return (returning, returned)
1 to come back or go back to a place
He returned after the meeting.
2 to give or send something back
We returned the books to the library.

rhinoceros
(rhinoceroses)
a very large, wild animal with thick skin and a large horn on its nose
Rhinoceroses have very weak eyesight.

▲ rhinoceros

rhyme (rhyming, rhymed)
when a word ends with the same sound as another word
Tree rhymes with three.

•Puzzle time•

Which words in column A rhyme with words in column B?

A	B
book	hard
card	boat
coat	look
cow	other
mother	so
sew	now

answers
book/look, card/hard,
coat/boat, cow/now,
mother/other, sew/so

ribbon
a narrow piece of cloth or paper for tying up presents or decorating things
What colour ribbon shall we put on her present?

▲ ribbon

rice
grains from a plant that are boiled and eaten as food
We had pilau rice with our vegetable curry.

▲ rice

rich
1 having a lot of money
We are not rich but we're very happy.
2 food that has butter, cream and eggs is rich food
The sauce is too rich for me!
3 a deep or strong colour, smell or sound
The queen is wearing rich, purple robes.

riddle
a difficult but funny question
Tom knows lots of riddles.

ride (riding, rode, ridden)
to travel on and control the movement of a bicycle or a horse
She is learning to ride a bike.

ride

right
correct
Well done — you got all the answers right!

ring
1 a piece of jewellery worn on the finger
It's a pretty silver ring.
2 a circle or something that is the shape of a circle
We put our chairs in a ring around the teacher.
3 the sound made by a bell
The phone has a very loud ring
4 a telephone call
Give me a ring when you get home from work.

river
a long line of water that flows to the sea.
The longest river in the world is the Nile.

road
a track for vehicles such as cars and trucks to travel on
Some country roads are very narrow.

roar
the sound a lion makes
There was a loud roar just outside the tent.

roar

robot
a machine that can do things that a person can do
My robot can play football.

robot

rock
1 the hard, stony part of the Earth's surface
They drilled through rock to find the oil.
2 a large stone
We sat on the rocks and fished.
3 a type of music that has a strong beat
My brother likes hard rock.

rocket
1 a space vehicle shaped like a tube
The rocket is carrying valuable equipment to the space station.
2 a tube-shaped firework
Rockets were exploding all over the sky.

rocket

roll (rolling, rolled)
to move by turning over
The ball rolled across the pitch.

roof
the outer covering over the top of a building or car
Rain leaked through the roof and onto the floor.

room
part of a building that has its own floor, walls and ceiling
What's your room like?

rope
very thick string
Tie the rope as tight as you can.

rope

rose
a flower that grows on a stem with thorns
My mother loves roses.

roses

rough
1 uneven, not smooth
That bench is quite rough.
2 not gentle
Don't be rough with the puppy.

roundabout
1 a round place where roads meet
Turn left at the next roundabout.
2 a round playground toy that children spin and ride on
Let's ride on the roundabout.

route
the way to go to a place
We looked at the map and decided which route to take.

row (rowing, rowed)
to move a boat through water using long poles that are wide at one end
We rowed across the lake.

royal
of or belonging to a queen or king
The royal palace is in the city.

rubber
1 a bouncy material that is made from the juice of a tree
Car tyres are made of rubber.
2 a small object used for taking marks off paper
Can I borrow your rubber?

rubbish
1 paper and other things that are no longer needed
When is the rubbish collected?
2 something that is bad, wrong or silly
The film was rubbish.

rude
speaking or acting in a way that makes people feel bad
It's rude to whisper.

rug
1 a small carpet
The dog is asleep on a rug.
2 a blanket
Put the rug over your feet.

rule
a law or guide about how something must be done
It's wrong to break the rules at school.

ruler
1 a long, flat piece of plastic or wood that has a straight edge and measurements on it
Use a ruler to draw a line.
2 a person who has power over a country
The country had no ruler when the king died.

ruler

run (running, ran)
1 to move your legs faster than when you are walking
Run as fast as you can!
2 to control
The business is run from home.
3 to make a piece of equipment or a computer programme work
Run the computer programme.

run

Did you know?
The fastest human being can run at an amazing 37 kilometres per hour!

S s

sad
unhappy
What's happened?
You look so sad.

safe
not dangerous
Home is where you feel good
and safe.

sail
a large piece of strong
material attached to a boat
or ship, that catches the wind
and makes the boat move
across the water
The ship has many sails.

▼ **sails**

sail (sailing, sailed)
to travel across water in
a boat or ship
I am learning to sail a boat.

salad
vegetables or fruit mixed
together, usually
eaten raw
We'll have
a mixed
salad.

▼ **salad**

salt
very tiny grains which come
from sea water and rocks,
that are put on food to make
it taste good
This needs a little more salt.

same
not different or changed
Look, our clothes are exactly
the same.

sand
tiny pieces of crushed rock
The beach is covered in
beautiful, white sand.

sandwich (sandwiches)
two pieces of bread with
cheese, meat or vegetables
in between
We'll make some
sandwiches for the picnic.

▼ **sandwich**

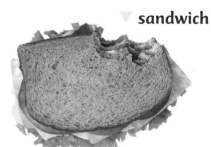

saucer
the small dish that goes under
a cup
We put some milk in a saucer
for the kittens.

sausage
a mixture of meat, cereal and
spices that is shaped like
a tube
Would you like sausages with
your breakfast?

scales
a machine that is used for
weighing things
Weigh the flour on the scales.

◄ **scales**

scar

the mark left on your skin after a cut has healed
I have a scar above my left eye.

scare (scaring, scared)

to frighten
The film will scare you.

scared

feeling afraid, frightened
Please leave a light on, I'm scared of the dark.

scarecrow

an object made to look like a person that is put in fields to scare birds off so they don't eat the crops
Our scarecrow is made of straw.

school

the place where children go to study and be taught
I'm studying French at school.

science

the study of information about the world
Biology, physics and chemistry are all kinds of science.

score (scoring, scored)

to get points in a game
Goal! Goal! We've scored another goal!

scorpion

an animal that has eight legs and a tail
Scorpions have a painful sting.

▲ **scorpion**

• **Did you know?** •

Scorpions have been on the Earth a very long time - about 4 million years!

scratch (scratching, scratched)

1 to rub your skin with your fingers or nails
Don't scratch your face.
2 to damage an object by rubbing it with something
The stones scratched the car.

scream (screaming, screamed)

to make a loud noise when you are afraid, angry or hurt
She screamed loudly.

screen

1 the flat part of a computer or television that you look at
You're too close to the screen.
2 a flat piece of material for showing films on
The cinema has a wide screen.

sea

a large area of salty water, sometimes called the ocean
Look, you can see the sea from here.

seal

1 an animal that lives in the sea and eats fish
Seals are good swimmers and can dive underwater for a long time.
2 wax, plastic or paper that you break to open a container or a document
Do not buy this product if the seal is broken.

▲ **seals**

• **Did you know?** •

Seals can be found in all the world's oceans. They are fast swimmers and skilful hunters of fish and squid, although the leopard seal hunts mainly penguins. Seals can dive to great depths and stay underwater for long periods of time. Lake Baikal, in Siberia, Russia is a huge inland lake, and is home to the world's only freshwater seals.

secret
something that you do not
want other people to know
*Please don't tell anyone else —
it's a secret.*

see (seeing, saw, seen)
1 to use your eyes to look
We saw a deer.
2 to understand
See? This is how it works.
3 to watch
*Did you see that programme
on TV last night?*
4 to meet or visit someone
*We went to see Chloe in
hospital.*

seed
the part of a plant that a new
plant grows from
*Put the seeds in the ground and
water them.*

seeds

seesaw
a long board that is balanced
in the middle so that the ends
go up and down
*There's a seesaw in the
playground.*

send (sending, sent)
to make something go or be
taken to another place
I sent her an email yesterday.

sew (sewing, sewed, sewn)
to join cloth together with a
needle and thread
I'll sew the button on for you.

shade
1 where the sun is not shining
Sit in the shade of the umbrella.
2 a thing to stop light
Pull the shades.
3 a colour
That's a nice shade of green.

shade

shake (shaking, shook, shaken)
to move something up and
down or side to side quickly
Shake well before opening.

shampoo
soap for washing your hair
Did you bring the shampoo?

shape
the outline or form of a thing
What shape is it?

shark
a large fish with sharp teeth
*Some sharks can be dangerous
to humans.*

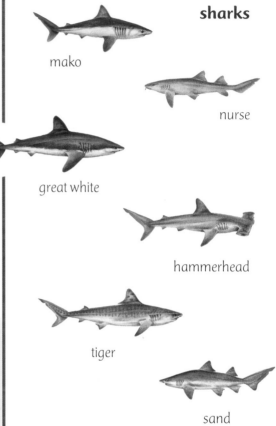
sharks
mako
nurse
great white
hammerhead
tiger
sand

sheep (sheep)
a farm animal kept for wool
and meat
There are sheep on the hill.

sheep

shelf (shelves)

a board, usually wooden, fixed on a wall for putting things on
Can you reach that shelf?

shell

the hard covering of an egg, a seed or an animal such as a turtle or a crab
Ostrich eggs are very big and have thick shells.

ship

a large boat
The pirates filled the ship with treasure.

ship

mizzen topsail
main topsail
mainsail
fore topsail
foresail
stern
sail locker
water and stores
oar
bow
bowsprit

· Did you know? ·

Pirate ships were small but fast. This meant they could make a quick getaway with stolen treasure.

shirt

a piece of clothing worn on the top half of your body
Tuck your shirt in.

shock

1 a bad surprise
The bill was quite a shock.
2 a pain you feel when electricity goes through your body
I got a shock from that plug!

shoe

one of the things made of strong material that you wear on your feet
Wear comfortable shoes.

shoot (shooting, shot)

1 to fire a weapon at someone or something
Don't shoot!
2 to kick or throw a ball into a goal or net in a game
Shoot when you are closer to the basket.

shop

a place that sells things
What time does the shop open?

short

1 not tall
He is short for his age.
2 not long
She cut her hair short.
3 not lasting a long time
Let's take a short break.

shorts

short trousers
We wear our shorts in summer.

shorts

shoulder

the top of your arm where it joins your body
Put the bag over your shoulder.

shout (shouting, shouted)
to call out in a loud voice
Don't shout, I'm right here!

show (showing, showed)
1 to let someone see something
Show me your new game.
2 to guide someone somewhere or help them to do something
The guide showed us around.

shower
1 a thing that you stand under to wash your body
Every room has a private shower.
2 a light fall of rain
There will be showers in the afternoon.

shrink (shrinking, shrank, shrunk)
to become smaller
My favourite skirt shrank in the wash.

shut (shutting, shut)
to close
Shut the door, please.

sideways
towards one side, not forwards or backwards
Turn sideways and then you can get past.

sign (signing, signed)
to write your name on something
Sign at the bottom.

silly
stupid, not reasonable
Don't be so silly!

sing (singing, sang, sung)
to make music with your voice
Sing us a song.

sink (sinking, sank, sunk)
to go down below the surface of water
'The Titanic' sank after it hit an iceberg.

▲ sink

sister
a girl or woman who has the same parents as you
Julie is my younger sister.

sit (sitting, sat)
to put your bottom on a chair or another type of seat
I must sit down, my feet ache.

skate (skating, skated)
to move over ground or ice wearing boots with wheels or blades
He can skate well.

▲ skate

skeleton
the bones in your body
He wore a suit with a skeleton painted on it for Hallowe'en.

sketch (sketching, sketched)
to draw quickly
Artists sketch a scene first.

ski (skiing, skied)
to move quickly over snow or water on long, narrow pieces of wood
Do you know how to ski?

▲ ski

skirt

a piece of clothing worn by girls and women that hangs from the waist down
You can wear that skirt to school.

sky (skies)

the space above you where the Sun, Moon, stars and clouds are
The sky was full of stars.

slap (slapping, slapped)

to hit something with an open hand
She slapped his hand.

sled (sledges)

a vehicle or toy for moving across ice or snow
We built a sled out of an old wooden box.

sleep (sleeping, slept)

to not be awake
The baby is sleeping in his cot.

▲ sleep

slide (sliding, slid)

to move across or down a smooth surface
The car slid across the ice.

slippers

shoes that you wear indoors
Put your slippers on if your feet are cold.

slow (slow)

not fast, taking a long time
This is a slow train.

small

little or young
The jeans have a small pocket for coins.

smile (smiling, smiled)

to make your mouth curve up and look happy
What are you smiling about?

▲ smile

smoke

the cloudy gas that is made when something burns
The room filled with smoke.

smooth

not rough or bumpy
You can skate on the pavement, it's smooth.

snail

an animal that looks like a worm with a shell on its back
We have a lot of snails in our garden.

▶ snail

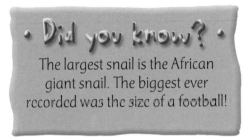

• Did you know? •

The largest snail is the African giant snail. The biggest ever recorded was the size of a football!

snake

an animal that has a long body with no legs
Simon has a pet snake.

▲ snake

sneeze (sneezing, sneezed)

to blow air out of your nose suddenly, with a loud noise
He's sneezing and coughing because he has a cold.

snow

soft pieces of frozen water
that fall from the sky
The trees are covered in snow.

snow

soap

something that you use with
water to wash your body
Get a new bar of soap.

soap

soccer

football, a game played by
two teams that try to get a
round ball between two posts
*There are eleven players on a
soccer team.*

soccer

socks

soft pieces of clothing that you
wear inside shoes
Socks keep your feet warm.

socks

sofa

a long, soft seat for two or
more people
Shall we sit on the sofa?

soft

1 not hard
These apples are a bit soft.
2 not loud
She has a soft voice.
3 smooth to touch
The rabbit has lovely, soft fur.

software

the programmes that run on
a computer
He designs software.

solid

hard, not a liquid or a gas,
without spaces inside
The front door is solid wood.

some

1 an amount that is not exact
Do you want some rice?
2 part of, but not all
Some of these apples are rotten.

son

a male child
His son is my age.

song

a piece of music
Let's all sing a song.

sore

hurting or painful
Is your leg still sore?

sorry

feeling bad and wanting to
apologise for something you
have done
I'm sorry I upset you.

soup

a liquid food made from meat
or vegetables
*Have a bowl of
tomato soup.*

soup

sour

having a taste like lemons,
not sweet
This juice is sour.

space

1 an empty or open place
Is there any space left?
2 everything outside the
Earth's air
Space travel is very exciting.

spade

a tool for digging
Turn the soil with a spade.

spaghetti

long, thin strips of pasta
Ella likes spaghetti.

spaghetti

speed

how fast something moves
At what speed are we travelling?

spell (spelling, spelled)

to write or say the letters of
a word in the correct order
How do you spell 'skateboard'?

spider

a small animal with
eight legs
*There's a spider in
the bath.*

spider

spill (spilling, spilled, spilt)

to cause a liquid to fall to the
ground accidentally
I spilled the drink on the carpet.

spoon

an object with a handle and
small bowl that is used
for eating
*Put the spoon to
the right of the
plate.*

spoon

sport

physical activities such as
swimming and tennis
*Swimming is a sport the
whole family likes.*

snowboarding

spring

the time of year between
winter and summer
*The cherry tree flowers
in spring.*

squirrel

a small wild animal with
a long, bushy tail
*Squirrels are very good
at climbing trees.*

sports

ice hockey

gymnastics

•Puzzle time•

Can you unscramble the names
of these sports?

a. gruyb **b**. gsmwmin
c. cykeoh **d**. nintes **e**. ftbllooa

answers
a. rugby b. swimming
c. hockey d. tennis e. football

volleyball

stairs
steps in a building that go from one floor to another
I'll take the stairs to the office.

stamp
1 a piece of paper that you buy to put on a letter or postcard before you post it
I'd like a first class stamp.
2 a thing you put ink on and then press onto something to make a mark
The letter has a stamp on it.

stand (standing, stood)
to be on your feet
She's standing by the door

star
1 a ball of burning gas that looks like a light in the sky
The stars are bright tonight
2 a famous actor or musician
She's a big star now.
3 a shape with five or six points
We baked biscuits shaped like stars

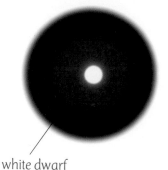

white dwarf

starfish (starfishes)
a star-shaped animal that lives in the sea
Starfish move very slowly.

◀ starfish

start (starting, started)
to begin
Ready? Let's start.

stay (staying, stayed)
1 to not leave a place
You stay here, I'll be right back.
2 to live in a place for a short amount of time
We stayed with my aunt for a week.
3 to continue to be the same
Stay happy!

steal (stealing, stole, stolen)
to take something that doesn't belong to you
The thief stole my dad's car.

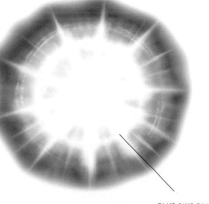

supernova

◀ stars

stick
a long, thin piece of wood
We made a fire by rubbing two sticks together.

stomach
the part inside your body where food goes when you eat it
Another word for stomach is tummy.

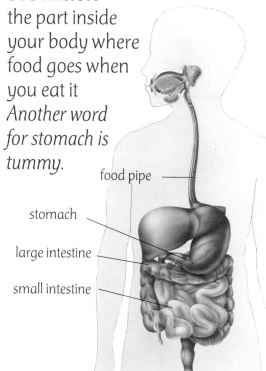

food pipe

stomach

large intestine

small intestine

▲ stomach

stone
1 rock
There is a stone floor in the castle.
2 fourteen pounds or 6.35 kilograms
What is your weight in stones?
3 the seed in some fruits
Careful, the cherries have stones in them.

stool
a seat with no back
We sit on stools in the art room.

stop (stopping, stopped)
1 to quit doing something
Stop talking for a minute.
2 to quit moving
You should stop for red lights.
3 to prevent something happening
The teacher stopped the fight.

story (stories)
a description of events that may be real or imaginary
Everyone knows the story of Peter Pan.

· Did you know? ·
The story about Peter Pan was first written by J.M. Barrie in 1902. Peter Pan was the hero in a novel called *The Little White Bird*. The story was then adapted for a play in 1904 called *Peter Pan*. In the play Peter flies away to Never Never Land, to avoid growing up. Other famous characters are the Darlings, Captain Hook and Tiger Lily.

straight
not crooked or bent
She has very straight hair.

strange
1 unusual
That's a strange-looking man.
2 unfamiliar
He told a very strange story.

strawberry (strawberries)
a soft, heart-shaped red fruit
You can pick the strawberries yourself on some farms.

▼ **strawberries**

stream
a small river
We drank water from a mountain stream.

stretch (stretching, stretched)
1 to get longer or bigger
Tights can stretch quite a bit.
2 to straighten parts of your body
She stretched her legs out under the table.

string
thick thread or thin rope
Tie some string around the box.

▲ **string**

strong
1 powerful
Climbers have strong legs.
2 not easily broken or damaged
The metal case is very strong.

stupid
not sensible or clever
What a stupid idea!

submarine
a ship that can travel underwater
Submarines can help us to find out about underwater life.

▲ **submarine**

sudden
happening quickly and unexpectedly
There was a sudden explosion.

sugar
a sweet substance used to
flavour food
Sugar is made from plants.

suitcase
a case or bag to carry clothes
in when you travel
We have a suitcase with wheels.

summer
the time of year between
spring and autumn
*Are you going on holiday this
summer?*

Sun
the very bright star that the
Earth travels around
*All the planets in the Solar
System travel around the Sun.*

Sun

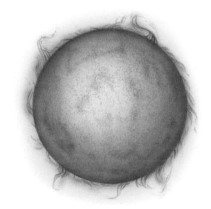

supermarket
a large shop that sells food
and other things
The supermarket is open.

surprise
something that is completely
unexpected
*An email from you! What a
nice surprise!*

sweep (sweeping, swept)
to brush dirt from the floor
or ground
Have you swept the kitchen?

sweet
1 tasting sugary
*These strawberries are very
sweet.*
2 nice or pleasant
That's a sweet thing to say.

swim (swimming, swam,
swum)
to move through or across
water by using your arms
and legs
*I can swim a a whole length of
the pool.*

swim

swing (swinging, swung)
to move backwards,
forwards or from side to side
from a fixed point
I like swinging, it's lots of fun.

swing

sword
a very large knife
that is used for
fighting
*'Excalibur' is the
name of a famous
sword.*

sword

Tt

T-shirt/t-shirt
a shirt with short sleeves, no collar and no buttons
Put a T-shirt on.

table
1 a piece of furniture with legs and a flat top
Please clear the table.
2 a list of things such as numbers or words arranged in rows and columns
There's a table of prices and times.

table

tail
the part of an animal at the end of its back
The dog has a long, white tail.

tail

take (taking, took, taken)
1 to carry something
Take an umbrella.
2 to move something or someone to another place
Take this note to Mrs. Burnett.
3 to steal
The thieves took all the money.

talk (talking, talked)
to speak
Who were you talking to?

tall
1 higher than normal
My Grandad is tall, I am short.
2 having a certain height
The fence is one metre tall.

tall

tank
1 a container for liquids
There's a leak in the petrol tank.
2 a large fighting vehicle
Tanks are used in wars.

tap
something that controls the flow of a liquid or gas
Turn the tap off.

tape
1 a long, flat, narrow piece of plastic used for recording sounds or images or the plastic container it is in
Can I borrow the tape?
2 flat, narrow plastic that is sticky on one side
Put some tape on the package.

taste (tasting, tasted)
1 to have a flavour
What does the soup taste like?
2 to try a little food or drink to see what it is like
Have you tasted the pizza?

taxi
a car that takes people places for money
We'll take a taxi.

taxi

tea
1 leaves that are used to make a drink or the drink made from these leaves
Pour the tea.
2 the evening meal
What's for tea?

teacher
a person who gives
lessons in a subject
Kate's an art teacher.

team
1 a group of people who
play a game together
Which team are you on?
2 a group of people who
work together on a project
We have a great team.

▲ **team**

tear
a drop of water that
comes out of your eye
Tears ran down his face.

tear (tearing, tore, torn)
to rip, split or make a hole
in something
Tear the paper in half.

teddy
a toy animal
that looks
like a bear
*My teddy is
soft and
cuddly.*

▲ **teddy**

telephone
a piece of equipment that
you use to speak to someone
in another place
Where's your telephone?

▲ **telephone**

telescope
a piece of equipment that
you use to look at things that
are far away
Look through the telescope.

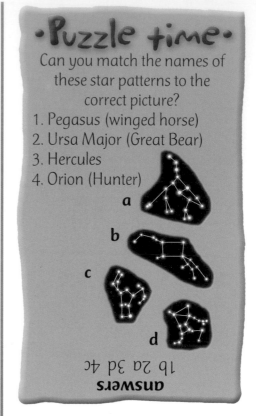
television (TV)
a machine that shows
programmes
What's on television?

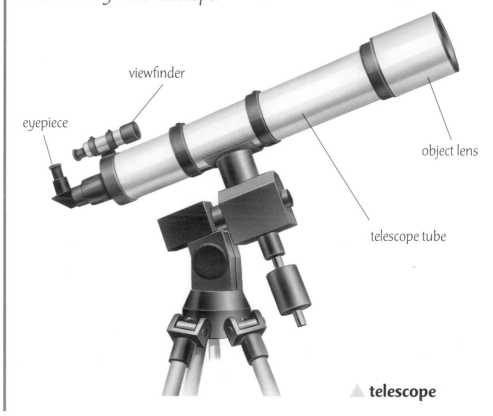

viewfinder

eyepiece

object lens

telescope tube

▲ **telescope**

a b c d e f g h i j k l m

tell (telling, told)
1 to pass on information
I told you that story yesterday.
2 to understand
I can't tell what it means.

tennis
a game played by two or four people who hit a ball over a net to score points
Tennis is a very fast game.

▲ tennis

tent
a temporary house, made of cloth or plastic, that is used for camping
The tent will keep us dry.

terrible
very bad
That's terrible!

test
1 a set of questions to measure knowledge
You must study carefully for the test.
2 a set of checks to find out if something is safe or good to use
Cars must pass several tests.

thank (thanking, thanked)
to tell someone you are pleased about something they have given you or have done for you
Remember to thank them.

theatre
a building where you can go and see plays
The Globe Theatre is round.

thick
1 not thin
The phone book is thick.
2 not watery
Make a thick paste from flour and water.

thief (thieves)
a person who steals
The thieves stole all the money from the bank.

thin
1 having not much distance from one side to the other
Cut thin strips of paper.
2 not fat
She's quite thin.
3 watery
It's a thin, clear soup.

think (thinking, thought)
1 to use your mind to consider or remember something
Let me think.
2 to have an opinion, to believe
I think we should try it.

thirsty
feeling that you need to drink something
Are you thirsty?

through
from one side to the other
Look through the window.

throw (throwing, threw)
to make something go through the air
Throw the ball through the net.

thumb
the finger on the inside of your hand
Use your thumb to hit the space bar on the keyboard.

thunder
the loud noise during a storm
*We heard a very loud clap
of thunder.*

ticket
a piece of paper that shows
you have paid
*Tickets are half price for
children.*

tidy
neat and organised
Mandy's room is never tidy.

·Puzzle time·

Can you spot six differences
between these two rooms?

answers
1 crumpled paper 2 spilled ink
3 sock 4 teddy 5 unmade bed
6 wardrobe door

tie (tying, tied)
to join pieces of string, rope
or thread together
Tie your shoe laces up.

tiger
a large, wild cat that has
black stripes on its yellow fur
Tigers are the biggest wild cats.

▼ **tiger**

· Did you know? ·
Tigers are the biggest cats but
there are few left in the wild. Over
hunting and destruction of their
habitat has made them very rare.

tight
1 close-fitting
That looks a bit tight.
2 firmly in place
Is it shut tight?

tights
clothing worn on the legs
I wear tights to ballet.

timetable
a list of things and the time
they happen
Check the timetable.

tired
feeling that you need to rest
The baby is tired.

toast
bread that has been cooked
in a toaster or a grill
*I'll make some toast for
breakfast.*

▲ **toast**

today
this day
What's the date today?

toe
one of the five parts of your
body at the end of your foot
Ouch, I stubbed my toe.

together
1 joined or mixed
Mix the eggs and milk together.
2 with each other
Shall we go together?

toilet
lavatory
Where's the toilet?

tomato (tomatoes)
a red fruit that
can be eaten
raw or
cooked
*Put tomatoes
in the salad.*

▲ **tomatoes**

tool

a piece of equipment that you use to do a job
Hammers and saws are tools.

tooth (teeth)

one of the hard, white things in your mouth
You should brush your teeth twice a day.

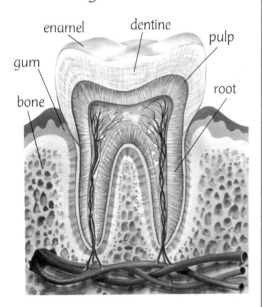

enamel   dentine   pulp
gum
bone   root

▲ **tooth**

tongue

the soft part of your body that is inside your mouth that you use to speak with and to taste things
The ice cream feels cold on my tongue.

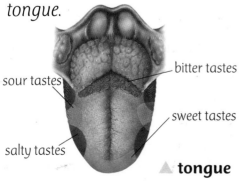

sour tastes   bitter tastes
sweet tastes
salty tastes

▲ **tongue**

top

1 the highest part of something
It's on top of the bookcase.
2 a toy that balances on a point
Let's spin the top.
3 a cover for the upper body
That's a pretty top.
4 a cover for a container
Put the top back on.

torch

a light powered by batteries
Shine the torch over here.

tortoise

a land animal that can pull its head and legs into the shell that covers its body
Tortoises are very slow-moving animals.

▼ **tortoise**

touch (touching, touched)

1 to put your fingers or hand on something
Don't touch the paintings.
2 to be so close to another thing that there is no space between the two
The wires are touching.

towel

a cloth that you use to dry things or your body with
Dry your hands on the towel.

town

a place with houses and other buildings where people live and work
A town is smaller than a city.

toy

something that children like to play with
Can I play with my toy plane?

◀ **toy**

tractor

a big vehicle that is used on a farm
Tractors are very powerful.

traffic lights

lights where two or more roads meet which change colour, telling you when to stop and go
Turn left at the traffic lights.

▶ **traffic lights**

train
a line of carriages pulled by an engine on a track
Trains travel at a fast speed.

trainers
sports shoes
I bought some new trainers.

▲ train

transport (transporting, transported)
to move people or things from one place to another
The tanker transports fuel.

trap (trapping, trapped)
to catch something in a piece of equipment
It traps mice.

travel (travelling, travelled)
to go from one place to another
They're travelling by car.

treasure
a collection of valuable things
The chest is filled with treasure.

▲ treasure

tree
a large, tall plant with a trunk and branches
It's fun to climb trees.

trick
1 something done to entertain people
That was a clever trick
2 something done to fool or cheat someone
That was a mean trick.

trip (tripping, tripped)
to catch your foot on something, to stumble
He tripped on the step.

trip
a journey
It's a short trip.

trousers
clothing worn on the lower half of the body, with separate places for each leg
He's wearing grey trousers.

truck
a vehicle for carrying loads
We were stuck behind a truck.

trunk
1 the main part of a tree
Palm trees have tall trunks.
2 an elephant's nose
The elephant has a long trunk.
3 a box for storing things in.
Where's the key for this trunk?

try (trying tried)
1 to make an effort to do or get something
I tried to ring you.
2 to test or sample something
Have you tried the pasta?

tunnel
a long hole underground
There is a secret tunnel.

turn
1 to move so you are looking or going in a new direction
He turned to look at us.
2 to move something to a different position
Turn the dial.

turtle
an animal that lives in water that can pull its head and legs into the shell on its back
Turtles are good swimmers.

▲ truck

a b c d e f g h i j k l m

ugly

not nice to look at
What an ugly colour!

umbrella

a piece of equipment made of cloth stretched over a frame that keeps the rain off
It's raining outside – I'll take my umbrella.

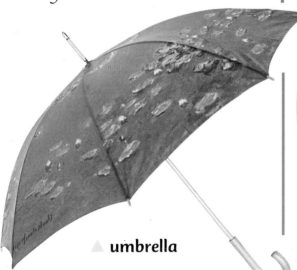

▲ umbrella

uncle

your mother's or father's brother, or your aunt's husband
He looks like his uncle.

under

below, to a lower place
Put your bag under your seat.

understand
(understanding, understood)
1 to know the meaning of words or ideas
Does he understand English?
2 to know how something works
Doctors understand the disease.
3 to know how and why someone feels or acts a certain way
You don't understand.

• Did you know? •

You can understand lots of words from other languages. The English language has borrowed words from many other languages
• From Italian we have words like: balcony, giraffe and violin.
• From Spanish we have banana and guitar.
• From French we have chocolate, crocodile and medicine.

underwear
pieces of clothing that you wear next to your body, under your other clothes
Pack some underwear.

unhappy
not happy, sad
Cheer up, try not to look so unhappy.

▶ unhappy

uniform
clothes worn by everyone in a group of people
Everyone wore uniforms.

▲ uniforms

up
towards a higher position
Pass that brush up to me.

upset
1 feeling worried, sad or angry
I didn't mean to upset you.
2 feeling sick
His stomach is upset.

upstairs
towards or on the upper floors of a building
Take these papers upstairs.

valley
the low land between two hills
there is a river in the valley.

van
a small truck
The delivery van is here.

vanish (vanishing, vanished)
to disappear
The deer suddenly vanished.

vase
a container to hold water in
The vase is hand-painted.

◀ vase

vegetable
a plant grown for food
Vegetables are healthy foods.

vehicle
a machine which carries
people or things
Trucks and trains are vehicles.

vest
an undershirt
Put a vest on, it's cold today.

vet (veterinary surgeon)
an animal doctor
The vet is treating our dog.

◀ vet

video (video cassette recorder)
a machine for recording or
playing TV programmes.
Switch the video on.

▲ video

village
a group of houses and
buildings in the country
It's a beautiful old village.

vinegar
a liquid that is used to
preserve food, or add flavour
Put vinegar on your chips.

violin
a musical
instrument that
is played with
a bow
*He's
learning
to play the violin.*

▲ violin

virus (viruses)
1 a very tiny living thing that
causes disease and illness
Flu is caused by a virus.
2 a computer programme
that can damage files
The virus has damaged my files.

visit (visiting, visited)
to go to see a person or
a place
You can visit us this evening.

voice
the sounds a person makes
when speaking or singing
I didn't recognise your voice.

volcano (volcanoes)
a mountain with an opening
that sprays out steam or lava
The volcano is very active.

vote (voting, voted)
to show which idea or person
you choose by raising your
hand or writing on paper
Let's take a vote on this.

Ww

waiter

a man or woman who serves food in a restaurant or café
Call the waiter, I want to pay.

▲ **waiter**

waitress

a woman who serves food in a restaurant or café
Ask the waitress for the bill.

wake (waking, woke, woken)

to stop being asleep
Wake up!

walk (walking, walked)

to move along, putting one foot in front of the other.
Let's walk together

• Puzzle time •

There are six words that start with 'W' in this puzzle. Can you find all of them? Words are written vertically ↑ and horizontally →

a	b	c	d	w	e	f
a	b	c	w	a	l	k
a	b	w	i	n	c	d
w	h	i	s	t	l	e
a	b	c	h	d	e	f
v	a	b	c	d	e	f
e	a	b	c	d	e	f

answers
walk wave want whistle win wish

---

wall

1 the sides of a room or a building
There are several pictures on the wall.
2 a structure made of stone or brick that divides a space
There's a brick wall around the garden.

wand

a magic stick that fairies, witches and magicians use to do magic tricks
She waved her wand and turned the pumpkin into a coach.

want (wanting, wanted)

to wish, desire or need something
Do you want a sandwich?

---

wardrobe

a cupboard to hang clothes in
It's a big wardrobe.

warm

slightly hot, not cool or cold
The water is lovely and warm.

wash (washing, washed)

to clean with water
Wash your face.

wasp

a black and yellow flying insect that stings
Wasps live in nests.

▲ **wasps**

wastepaper bin

a container to put unwanted paper and rubbish in
Empty the wastepaper bin.

watch

a small clock that you wear on your wrist.
I'd like a watch for my birthday.

watch (watching, watched)

to look at something and pay attention
We're watching TV.

water

a liquid which falls from the sky as rain
Have a glass of water.

---

waterfall

water from a stream or a river that falls straight down over rocks
There is a pool under the waterfall.

▲ **waterfall**

wave

1 a raised part of moving water on the sea
Waves crashed on the beach.
2 a movement of your hand to say goodbye, hello or get someone's attention
Give them a wave.
3 the way light and sound move
The sound of the music is carried on radio waves.

▼ **wave**

weak

not strong
I feel weak and dizzy.

wear (wearing, wore)

to have something, such as clothes, on your body
What shall I wear to the party?

weather

the condition of the air – how hot or cold it is, the wind, rain and clouds
What's the weather like today?

web

1 the very thin strings a spider weaves
A spider catches food in its web.
2 the World Wide Web on the Internet
Do you use the Web?

•Puzzle time•

Tarantulas are big, hairy spiders that live in hot countries. Their bite can kill small animals.

tarantula

How many words of three letters and above can you make from 'tarantula'? You should be able to make at least 10.

week

seven days
See you next week!

weigh (weighing, weighed)

1 to measure how heavy something is
Weigh the fruit.
2 to be heavy or light
How much do you weigh?

well

1 in a good way
Well done!
2 healthy, not ill
Get well soon.

wet

not dry
Your hair's still wet.

whale

a very large sea animal
Whales are mammals, not fish.

▼ **whale**

wheel

a round object that turns and moves a vehicle along
The wheel came off the bike.

whisper (whispering, whispered)

to speak very quietly so other people can't hear
Whisper the secret to me.

whistle (whistling, whistled)
to blow air out through your lips and make a sound
Can you whistle?

wicked
very bad or evil
The wicked witch trapped them.

wife (wives)
the woman that a man is married to
His wife is very nice.

win (winning, won)
to be the first or the best in a race or other competition
He's won the race!

▲ win

wind
air moving across the ground
The wind is strong.

window
a glass-covered opening in a building
Look out of the window.

winter
the time of year between autumn and spring
The weather can be very cold in winter.

▲ winter

wish (wishing, wished)
to hope for or want something
What did you wish for?

•Puzzle time•
Use the code to find out what someone has wished for

A	B	C	D	E	F	G	H	I	J
1	2	3	4	5	6	7	8	9	10

K	L	M	N	O	P	Q	R
11	12	13	14	15	16	17	18

S	T	U	V	W	X	Y	Z
19	20	21	22	23	24	25	26

1 14/5/23 2/9/11/5

answer
a new bike

witch (witches)
a woman who is supposed to have magic powers
The witches huddled over their big, black pot, making spells.

▲ witches

• Did you know? •
Witches have been around for thousands of years. Originally, witchcraft was an ancient religion. In the Middle Ages, many people were burnt at the stake, accused of being witches. Modern witches do exist, but they do not fly on broomsticks!

wizard
a man who is supposed to have magic powers
The wizard broke the spell.

▲ wizard

wolf (wolves)

a wild animal that looks like
a large dog
*They heard the wolf howling
at the moon.*

▶ **wolf**

woman (women)

a female adult
Are there women on the team?

wonder (wondering, wondered)

to think about something
and why it is that way
I wonder why she said that?

wood

1 the material that a tree is
made of
Put more wood on the fire.
2 a small forest
We walked through the wood.

wool

1 hair that grows on
animals, such as sheep.
The wool is thick and warm.
2 thread made from this hair
Get me a ball of wool.

worry (worrying, worried)

to have the feeling that
something bad might happen
*You shouldn't worry, it's not
a problem.*

work (working, worked)

1 to do a job
*Does she enjoy her work as
a doctor?*
2 to go or operate smoothly
*This machine is working
properly now.*

• Puzzle time •

See if you can match the
workers with the things they
need to do their jobs.

A	B
actor	paint
artist	theatre
barber	menu
pilot	scissors
waiter	plane

answers
actor/theatre, artist/paint,
barber/scissors, pilot/plane,
waiter/menu

world

the Earth, the planet that we
live on and everything that
is on it
*The Nile is the longest river in
the world.*

worm

a long, thin animal with no
legs that
lives in
earth
*Worms
are good
for the soil.*

▲ **worm**

• Did you know? •

The Gippsland giant worm
is a 4-m-long Australian
earthworm. It makes
a slurping, gurgling sound
as it slides its way through
its burrow.

worse (worst)

also see bad
*That is the worst song on
the CD.*

write (writing, wrote)

1 to make a new story, poem,
play, song or book
*I wrote an exciting story at
school.*
2 to make letters, numbers
and words
Write your name in the diary.

wrong

not right, incorrect
We made a wrong turn.

x-ray

1 a beam of energy that can go through solid things
X-rays are used at airports.
2 a photograph of the inside of the body
The x-ray shows that his hand may be broken.

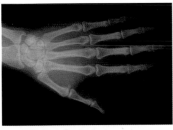
▶ **x-ray**

xylophone

a musical instrument that is played by hitting flat, wooden or metal bars with a pair of sticks
The word xylophone comes from the Greek words 'xylo' (wood) and 'phone' (sound).

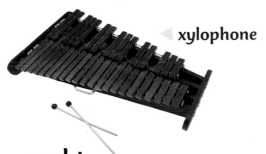
▶ **xylophone**

yacht

a sailing boat
Yacht races are exciting.

◀ **yacht**

yawn (yawning, yawned)

to open your mouth and take a deep breath, usually when you are tired or bored
I can't stop yawning – I'm going to bed.

year

a period of time that is equal to twelve months, especially from January to December
We're moving to a new house early next year.

yes

a word that is used to say that you want something, that you will do something, that you agree with something or that something is true
Would you like another slice of pizza? Yes, please!

yesterday

the day before today
I phoned you yesterday.

yo-yo

▼ **yo-yo**

a toy that moves up and down on a string that you hold in your hand
This yo-yo glows in the dark.

yoga

exercises for your body and mind
Yoga comes from India.

yoghurt (yogurt)

a food made from milk
I'd like a strawberry yoghurt.

young

not old
The dog is still very young.

zebra

a wild, black and white striped animal that looks like a horse
Zebras live in Africa.

▲ **zebras**

zero

nothing, 0
The temperature is zero degrees.

zip

a fastener made of two rows of teeth which lock together
This case needs a new zip.

zoo

a place where wild animals are kept so that people can look at them and study them
We went to the zoo.

Useful lists of words

Days of the week

Monday
Tuesday
Wednesday
Thursday
Friday
Saturday
Sunday

Months of the year

January
February
March
April
May
June
July
August
September
October
November
December

Numbers

1	one	first
2	two	second
3	three	third
4	four	fourth
5	five	fifth
6	six	sixth
7	seven	seventh
8	eight	eighth
9	nine	ninth
10	ten	tenth
11	eleven	eleventh
12	twelve	twelfth
13	thirteen	thirteenth
14	fourteen	fourteenth
15	fifteen	fifteenth
16	sixteen	sixteenth
17	seventeen	seventeenth
18	eighteen	eighteenth
19	nineteen	nineteenth
20	twenty	twentieth
21	twenty-one	twenty-first
22	twenty-two	twenty-second
23	twenty-three	twenty-third
24	twenty-four	twenty-fourth
25	twenty-five	twenty-fifth
26	twenty-six	twenty-sixth
27	twenty-seven	twenty-seventh
28	twenty-eight	twenty-eighth
29	twenty-nine	twenty-ninth
30	thirty	thirtieth
40	forty	fortieth
50	fifty	fiftieth
60	sixty	sixtieth
70	seventy	seventieth
80	eighty	eightieth
90	ninety	ninetieth
100	one hundred	hundredth
101	one hundred and one	one hundred and first
1,000	one thousand	thousandth
1,000,000	one million	millionth

Colours

red
orange
yellow
green
blue
indigo
violet

▲ rainbow colours

Other colours we see and use

purple
pink
grey
cream
brown
white
black
turquoise
lilac

Shapes

triangle

circle

oval

square

rectangle

diamond

pentagon

hexagon

octagon

semicircle

Measurements of length

millimetre (mm)
centimetre (cm) = 10 mm
metre (m) = 100 cm
kilometre (km) = 1,000 m

Measurements of weight

milligram (mg)
gram (g) = 1,000 mg
kilogram (kg) = 1,000 g
tonne (t) = 1,000 kg

Our world

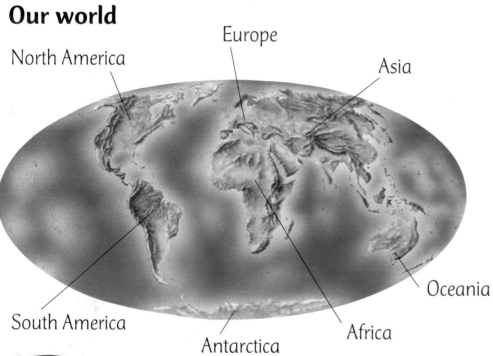

North America
Europe
Asia
Oceania
South America
Africa
Antarctica

Time

o'clock	of the clock
quarter past	fifteen minutes past the hour
half past	thirty minutes past the hour
quarter to	fifteen minutes until the next hour

Seasons

Spring

Summer

Autumn

Winter

Words that we use all the time

Here is an alphabetical list of words you use all the time. This list will help you check your spelling.

Aa
accident
add
aeroplane
afraid
afternoon
again
also
angry
animal
another
answer
any
apple
asleep
away

Bb
baby
back
bad
bag
ball
balloon
bat
bath
beautiful
because
bed
begin
behind
below
between
bicycle
big
birthday
body
book
boy
bring
brother
build

Cc
cake
call
can
car
careful
cat
CD
chair
change
chocolate
choice
cinema
clever
climb
clock
close
clothes
coat
cold
colour
computer
count

could
cry

Dd
dad
dance
daughter
day
die
difficult
dinner
dinosaur
disk
doctor
dog
door
down
draw
dress
drink
drive
dry

Ee
ear
early
easy
eat
egg
email
end
enjoy
enough
except
eye

Ff
face
fall
family
far
faraway
farm
fast
feel
fill
find
fire
floor
follow
food
football
forget
forwards
free
friend
frighten
front
fruit
full
fun
funny

Gg
garden
ghost
girl

give
good
goodbye
great
grow

Hh
hair
hamburger
hand
happen
happy
hate
head
hear
heavy
hello
help
here
hide
high
hill
hit
hold
holiday
home
homework
hope
horrible
hospital
hot
hour
hungry
hurry
hurt

Ii
ice
ice cream
idea
important
inside
interesting
Internet
its
it's

Jj
jacket
jam
job
join
joke
juice
jump
jumper
just

Kk
keep
kettle
key
keyboard
kick
kill
kind
kiss

kitchen
know
knew

Ll
lamp
large
last
late
laugh
learn
leave
let
library
lie
light
like
listen
little
long
look
loose
lose
loud
love
lovely
lucky
lunch

Mm
machine
magic
make
man
mean
meat
medicine
meet
middle
milk
minute
mirror
miss
mobile phone
money
monitor
monster
more
morning
move
much
mum
music
must

Nn
name
naughty
near
never
new
news
next
nice
night
nobody
noise
none
no one
nothing
now
number

Oo
off
often
OK (okay)
old
once
open
ordinary
out
outdoors
over
own

Pp
pack
page
pain
paint
pair
paper
park
part
party
pass
passed
past
pay
pen
pencil
person
pet
phone
photo
picture
piece
place
plane
play
playground
please
police
pool
poor
present
pretend
pretty
price
printer
problem
pull
puppy
push
put

Qq
quarter
queen
question
queue
quick
quickly
quiet
quite
quilt

Rr
race
radio
rain
read
remember
remind

repeat
rest
return
rich
ride
right
ring
road
room
rubbish
run

Ss
sad
safe
same
sandwich
school
screen
sea
secret
see
send
shape
shoe
shop
shout
show
shut
sing
sister
sit
sky
sleep
slow
smile
sneeze
snow
socks
some
song
sorry
spell
stand
start
stay
stop
story
strong
suddenly
sun
surprise
swim

Tt
table
take
talk
tall
tea
teacher
teddy
telephone
television (TV)
tell
thank
their
there
think
thought
through
tired

together
toilet
top
touch
toy
tree
try

Uu
ugly
umbrella
under
understand
unhappy
uniform
up
upset
upstairs

Vv
van
vegetable
video
village
visit
voice

Ww
wake
walk
wall
want
warm
wash
watch
water
wave
weather
week
weigh
well
wet
wheel
whisper
who's
whose
win
wind
window
wish
wonder
wood
work
world
would
write
wrong

XxYyZz
x-ray
yawn
year
yes
yesterday
young
zebra
zip
zoo

The publishers would like to thank the following artists who have contributed
to this book:

Lisa Alderson, Julie Banyard, Martin Camm, Jim Channell,
Kuo Kang Chen, Mark Davis, Nicholas Forder, Mike Foster, Luigi Gallante,
Peter Gregory, Alan Hancocks, Ron Haywood, Sally Holmes, Richard Hook,
Rob Jakeway, Tony Kenyon, Sue King, Steve Kirk, Mick Loates, Kevin Madison,
Alan Male, Janos Marffy, Josephine Martin, Tracy Morgan, Gill Platt, Terry Riley, Andy Robinson,
Mike Saunders, Peter Sarson, Rob Sheffield, Guy Smith, Roger Smith,
Mike Taylor, Peter Taylor, Mike White, Colin Woolf

The publishers would like to thank Ted Smart for the generous loan of his illustrations

The publishers would like to thank the following for supplying photographs for this book:
Corbis: Reuters New Media 133 (c/l)

All other pictures from the Miles Kelly Archives